Computers and Writing

Theory, Research, Practice

Edited by

Deborah H. Holdstein

Cynthia L. Selfe

———◆———

The Modern Language Association of America
New York   1990

Library of Congress Cataloging-in-Publication Data

Computers and writing : theory, research, practice / edited by Deborah H. Holdstein,
  Cynthia L. Selfe.
      p.   cm.
    Includes bibliographical references.
    ISBN 0-87352-193-5   ISBN 0-87352-194-3 (pbk.)
    1. English language – Composition and exercises – Study and teaching – Data process-
ing. 2. English language – Rhetoric – Study and teaching – Data processing. 3. Computer-
assisted instruction. 4. Word processing in education. I. Holdstein, Deborah H., 1952–
II. Selfe, Cynthia L., 1951– .
    PE1404.C6325   1990
    808'.042'0285 – dc20   89-77312

Published by The Modern Language Association of America
10 Astor Place, New York, New York 10003-6981

Contents

Introduction

Deborah H. Holdstein and Cynthia L. Selfe

Although English professionals will find a number of new books about computers on the lists of their favorite publishers, this collection of essays on computers differs from its competitors in fundamental ways. Our purpose is not to advise English teachers on appropriate ways of using the computer in their classes but rather to identify, examine, and analyze a broad range of computer-based issues in English departments and programs. We do not tell instructors "how to." Instead, we want to make professionals think "what about . . . ?"

The collection also differs from most similar works because it takes a "second generation" view of issues surrounding computer use in departments of English and the humanities. The thinking represented by the volume grows out of a healthy skepticism about computers that marks our more developed understanding of the technology – a position contrasting dramatically with our profession's initial flurry of blind enthusiasm. The serious, legitimate concerns identified by the contributors to this collection serve as an intellectual counterbalance to the bandwagon approach that characterized our early adoption of computers in college English classrooms and departments during the first six years of the 1980s.

In the issues that link them and those that divide them, the essays included here offer a sampling of current thinking about computers and composition, an area that has come into its own as a forum for theoretical, interpretive speculation as well as pedagogy. Taking what was previously perceived as a skill- and pedagogy-bound area to spheres of inquiry that still inform the classroom, the essays explore its political implications, debate numerous valid, if conflicting, views, and consider the appropriate "next phase" of investigation beyond (but not necessarily without) classroom practice.

In doing so, the authors address a variety of important issues: for instance, the need for theory and the connections between critical theory and other multidisciplinary contexts as influences toward that theory (and resulting practice). In grounding our teaching in theory, we can begin to see the ways in which other disciplines help develop theory based in computers and composition and the implications of that work. Yet conducting scholarly work in the field bears implications for one's professional status and the ways in which composition faculties' talents in the field are used within an English department, a situation requiring faculty members and administrators to unite to dispel the myths of computer use within the curriculum. For instance, the ability to "publish" on networks will eventually change the ways in which colleagues are reviewed for tenure and promotion and in turn will raise additional issues of access to published materials and an author's privacy. Whither the tenure portfolio as we know it – and its contents?

As more students learn to use computers to support their writing, we must consider those who are more frequently denied than granted access. An awareness of such ethical issues as equality of access suggests that technology bestows political power on those who master it – or, more accurately, on those who have the opportunity to master it – and obliges us to address those issues as regularly as we might schedule computer laboratory time. Similarly, we will have to augment our college-level teacher-training efforts as theoretical perspectives within and outside composition as a discipline begin to inform our practice, helping our students become empowered by technology as they become empowered by language.

While our authors raise significant issues such as these, they cannot provide solutions as readily as one could to the problems we posed five or six years ago: Crowding in the lab? Put a peer revision group approach to work! Where once scholar-teachers sought clear evidence that computer use improved written products, they now realize how simplistic their expectations were. The perspectives they offer have now become "givens"; several research studies in this field indicate that the computer does not in itself contribute to higher quality in written documents (Hawisher, "Effects"; Etchison) but that social and political environments, hardware, software, pedagogy, and attitudes toward computers figure prominently in any discussion of technology's effects. Other writing specialists, moreover, have begun to see that computer environments must accommodate writers in addition to traditional computer users (Holdstein and Redman; Selfe and Wahlstrom, "Computers") and that teachers must accompany computer use with creative and effective pedagogical approaches and technologically based writing strategies (Holdstein, *On Composition*).

Because complex issues surround the use of computers in English classrooms, we cannot rely solely on the isolated experiments and observations we have conducted in our own classrooms to inform our use of computers or to direct the integration of technology in our curricula and professional lives. Certainly, as Kathleen Kiefer writes, "we need to keep asking questions" ("Revising" 27) in our teaching and our scholarship.

Although we did not demand this of individual writers, the essays comment and expand on issues implied or suggested by the others. The first, Thomas Barker's "Computers and the Instructional Context," considers the pedagogical and logistical implications of introducing computers into writing classes and programs. Barker first examines traditional attitudes that shape and influence curricula within English departments and then explores how some of the myths concerning computers have contributed to a narrowly held view of their use in writing programs. In addition, Barker outlines three significant issues that will determine our profession's future success with computers: teacher training, teachers' attitudes toward computers, and the roles of teachers and students in connection with computers.

When the computer becomes part of the writing curriculum, ethical issues take on particular significance. Although the new technology in and of itself may seem value-free, its application entails implicit ethical choices, including those involving class, race, and gender. In "Ethical Considerations of Educational Computer Use," Helen J. Schwartz discusses three areas that raise ethical questions unique to computer use in writing classes and programs: the design and classroom use of software, the distribution of software, and student access to computers. Schwartz identifies the political and ethical aspects of these issues and notes that the responsibility for addressing them lies with the society that designs the educational context in which they occur.

Any ethical judgments about the use of computers in the teaching of writing presupposes some theoretical interpretation of the relation between computers and writing – that is, between the technology and the human activity. Ethical judgments are hermeneutical in that they are necessarily about an object under interpretation; all activities and objects are interpreted and can never be neutral. Discussing the influence of recent critical theory and other theoretical perspectives toward the relation of computers and composition, Deborah H. Holdstein acknowledges in "A Theory of One's Own? An Introduction to Theoretical and Critical Contexts for Computers and Composition" that, ultimately, theory might (and must) generate from the computers and from composition itself. Holdstein argues that a strong theoretical base not only fosters developments in research and teaching but also enhances the position, within the academy, of computers and composition – and, by implication, for those teaching and writing about the field as a whole.

David N. Dobrin, in "A Limitation on the Use of Computers in Composition," makes a theoretical distinction between two kinds of meaning in any text: the meaning that can be created by the organization within a sentence and the meaning that is created by the organization of a text – the structure, the organization of collected sentences. Addressing the controversial issue of using computers to analyze texts in English classes, Dobrin maintains that those programs designed to analyze the expression of meaning are not useful now and will not be useful because of the inevitable inaccuracy of computer-based language manipulation. From within the context of theories that regard the making of meaning – logically, grammatically, and rhetorically – as social and therefore political, Michael Spitzer, in "Local and Global Networking: Implications for the Future," looks at how the power of electronic networks can be exploited to support a socially based view of composition pedagogy.

Since teachers of writing will be expected to use computer technology, they must learn not only how it works but how they can integrate theoretical, ethical, and political perspectives to evaluate the effectiveness of their practice. In "Reading and Writing Connections: Composition Pedagogy and Word Processing," Gail E. Hawisher examines the role of in-service training programs in determining the uses of computers in English classes. Noting that teachers must be trained to make sound decisions about the integration of computer technology into their class-rooms, Hawisher offers a model in-service workshop designed to provide them with the strategies they need for an effort bearing ever-widening implications.

As indicated by the publication, in 1987, of Gerald Graff's *Professing Litera-ture*, institutional philosophies influence the political issues within a department and the types of research and pedagogy that are rewarded or rejected by the depart-ment. Research on the place of the computer in the teaching of writing has had an impact – on promotion, tenure, and reappointment; on departmental social sys-tems; on publication; on research itself; and on the way in which we see the fu-ture of composition studies and the profession as a whole. In this light, Ellen McDaniel explores the functions and responsibilities of computer experts in the English department. In "Assessing the Professional Role of the English Depart-ment 'Computer Person,'" McDaniel advocates "responsible discussion" by depart-mental and institutional-level administrators about what experts to hire, how such individuals should be compensated, and what scholarly activities they should be expected to produce. She notes that computer experts, as individuals who have only recently been hired by humanities departments, whose teaching is nontradi-tional, and whose research is unfamiliar, are "among those [faculty members] who can be victimized by the established categories and measures of evaluation in tradi-tional English and humanities departments."

Discussing the computer's impact on existing social systems of the department, as if to take the notion of institutional (here, departmental) philosophies in an-other direction, Cynthia L. Selfe argues in "Computers in English Departments: The Rhetoric of Techno/Power" that the value of technology may reside as much in its power as a tool of social reform as it does in its power as a tool of communi-cation. Used with a humanistic instinct, Selfe notes, computers can support the notion of English departments as social collectives, intellectual communities that revolve around a common set of goals. And in "Who Profits from Courseware?" Lisa Gerrard addresses the twin issues of software authorship and ownership – that would appear to contradict the leanings of most literature- and criticism-based departments of English – for teachers of English who set out to develop their own computer-based courseware. As the market for educational software has grown, according to Gerrard, so has its potential to generate income for English-instructor software authors. Although, she reminds us, educational software is unlikely to prove as lucrative as commercial packages (such as *Wordstar* or *Microsoft Word*), the prospect of financial return has interested authors and their institutional spon-sors in marketing ventures. It has also raised difficult questions about ownership and royalties (and the perceptions of that kind of work) that both parties must resolve.

In another essay treating an aspect of inquiry with implications for institutional philosophy – and yet stemming from the context of that philosophy – Andrea W.

Herrmann discusses the impact of computers on the research agendas of English professionals. In "Computers and Writing Research: Shifting Our 'Governing Gaze,'" Herrmann notes that although research on the effects of computers as writing tools has increased dramatically since the mid-1980s, English educators still lack a clear perception of the role computers play, or are capable of playing, in the writing process and the teaching of writing. She suggests that to obtain a more accurate understanding of the impact computer technology has on writing, we must seek a macrocosmic rather than a microcosmic view of our work, seeing our research as a way of formulating important questions and giving us a clearer view of possible directions for research.

We need look no further than our own professional backyard for evidence of the changes that computer technology has wrought. Having already committed itself to computer-related publications, the Modern Language Association's Fall 1987 *Newsletter* details its own advances for the scholar:

> Slowly but surely, we are witnessing a change in the way research is conducted in the humanities, and the availability of personal computers equipped with telecommunications software and modems will continue to increase the individual scholar's ability to take advantage not only of MLA Online but also of the hundreds of other databases currently available. (17)

In 1978, the *MLA Bibliography* became available for online use; now the MLA joins science database producers by providing CD-ROM (compact disk, read-only memory) for *Bibliography* users. But even these scholarly applications of computers have disadvantages: the need to regulate standards for encoding data; problems of equipment compatibility; for now, the relatively high cost (17–18). Obviously, too, ethical issues of access and power apply: What is the potential impact for faculty at institutions that cannot afford the latest technology on which we offer our scholarly apparatus?

Other changes at the MLA may be more heartening to readers: the scholarly organization boasts an MLA-IBM software initiative, one that reviews educational software pertaining to the study of modern languages and literature. That our traditionally minded organization has committed so many of its resources and energies to technology indicates the topic's potential for acceptance within the scholarly community as a whole. Even more recently, scholars in two related organizations, the Conference on College Composition and Communication and the National Council of Teachers of English, have begun to call for a nationwide computer network that would link English instructors, scholars, and researchers at all levels.

But the transition to a technologically supported and electronically connected profession has only started, and no one should expect it to progress without a number of false starts. Clearly, the contributors to this volume have identified many of the important questions that will face such a networking movement. Even when the issues themselves seem without controversy, they are not, and it is dangerous for faculty members to imply that they are. Furthermore, the ways in which practical, ethical, and pedagogical dilemmas might be resolved for the college-level English department suggest other serious implications for any writer, whether student or professor.

Our charge as teachers of writing makes us particularly responsible, if not for finding the answers to these questions, then for raising them, making sure that they are heard, and, most significant, for contributing to their equitable resolution. In writing these essays, the authors suggest not only that there are connections between computers and writing, philosophies of learning, and philosophies of institutions but also that pedagogy is as essential a component of good theory as a theoretical underpinning is to effective pedagogy.

We wish to acknowledge the support and the assistance of the MLA, particularly Adrienne Marie Ward, a capable and patient editor; Walter S. Achtert; Claire Cook; and Elizabeth Holland. We also wish to thank Roger Gilman, a Northeastern Illinois University faculty member in philosophy, for offering insightful comments on the introduction; and Richard Selfe, for lending his expertise on people and computers to Cynthia Selfe for her essay.

Computers and the Instructional Context

Thomas T. Barker

———◆———

Commentaries on the use of computers and word processors in composition instruction generally fall into one of the following broad categories: (1) analyses of the transition from pen-and-pencil composition to word processing or computer assistance, (2) examinations of research into the effect of computers on all phases of writing instruction, (3) descriptions of the uses of computers in classroom and lab settings, and (4) descriptions of computer-assistance programs by developers of those programs. We are beginning to see, however, an increasing number of essays that address larger concerns – such issues as teachers' roles, political considerations, and curriculum design. Helen J. Schwartz's "Monsters and Mentors," for example, was the first article to point out that computers challenge our traditional roles as teachers and researchers. Other writers have raised questions about such issues as the quality of computer-assisted instruction, the usefulness of empirical research in word processing and writing, problems in software development, and the role of computers in professional advancement (Holdstein and Redman; Barker, "Issues"; Burns, "Pandora's Chip"; Bourque). These and other essays are helpful to English teachers because they question the value of computers as educational tools and they expose some of the realities of our now middle-aged love affair with the electronic writing machine.

Despite the flurry of books and articles about computers, the effect of computers on our thinking about classroom activities has received limited attention. Essays about "integrating" computers into classroom teaching tend merely to recount one person's or one department's initial experiences (Dinan, Gagnon, and Taylor; Marcus, "Real-Time"), or they suggest ways to invent computerized writing activities for classroom instruction. Useful though these articles are, they do not usually address the long-range effect of computers on theories of classroom teaching – that is, our thinking about such issues as teacher training, teachers' attitudes, and teachers' and students' roles.

Traditionally these issues have been related to the instructional context. By "instructional context," researchers have meant the environment – classroom, lab, home, office, dorm room – where composing, revising, and proofreading take place and, on a larger scale, the institutional structure surrounding the writing. As Lillian Bridwell and Richard Beach have noted, concerns about instructional context relate to our application of research to practice. Practical results in the instructional context justify research; conversely, good teaching practices need to be grounded on evidence from research.

Evidence suggests that the computer will have a lasting and deep effect on the instructional context. Cynthia L. Selfe, in "Creating a Computer Lab," approaches the issues of the privacy of students' texts and lab design for writing. Thomas Barker, in "Issues in Software Development in Composition," examines the effect of computers on the teaching environment and teachers' roles. Studies of collaborative writing also consider some of the ways in which computers are reshaping our classrooms, and our roles in them (Herrmann, "Interim Report"; Bernhardt and Appleby; Selfe, "Dancing"). In her book *Writing and Computers*, Collette Daiute notes that the computer's "entry into the classroom involves design issues with logistical and pedagogical implications" (283).

The purpose of this essay is to explore some of these implications. First, I will look at some of our traditional attitudes toward the instructional context, to review briefly how some of the myths about computers and writing may have contributed to a narrow concept of their use. Then I will outline three main issues regarding computers in the classroom: teacher training, teachers' attitudes, and teachers' and students' roles. My intention is to reveal some of the exciting possibilities that have been uncovered so far and to clarify some of the issues surrounding the use of computers in classrooms. At times I have sacrificed detailed, focused analysis for the sake of presenting a broad overview of some complex issues. It is my hope that this overview will help teachers who face the challenge of adapting computers to the writing classroom.

Misconceptions about the Use of Computers in Classroom Teaching

Because teaching styles vary, with no proof that any one style works better than another, a gifted lecturer may motivate students as effectively as a teacher who has a talent for conducting writing conferences. The importance of a teacher's personal style cannot be overestimated. Joseph Axelrod, in *The University Teacher as Artist*, acknowledges this fact in his discussion of styles of teaching. His classification of teaching modes helps us understand some of the traditional attitudes toward classroom teaching, attitudes that shape our view of computers (7–16).

One mode Axelrod describes puts the teacher at the center of classroom activity. "Instructor-centered" teaching, as Axelrod calls it, evokes the image of the teacher at the front of the room and the students in rows of desks; the teacher, the indispensable controller of knowledge, disseminates it to the students, much as a farmer might sow seeds. In this role the teacher might prepare the ground by using remediation, to fertilize it and make it better able to accept and nurture the seeds. What this mode often impedes is the recognition or self-discovery of knowledge by students, from books, from their experiences, and so on.

Most of us have, at one point or another, seen ourselves in this role. With certain subject matter or under certain situations, it can be highly productive. Unfortunately, the instructor-centered mode of teaching fosters the myth that computers are used primarily for remediation, for bringing students up to speed in an area in which they are deficient. At its worst, this approach to instruction encourages us to see computers as bad imitations of teachers, as machines that lead students through tedious drill-and-practice exercises. A number of microcomputer facilities in colleges and universities employ computers in this way; the 1986 *English Microlab Registry* records the use of drill-and-practice software in about twenty percent of its labs ("Microlab"). However, most of these facilities are learning-assistance centers, whose expressed purpose is remediation and for which the computer may function productively as a teaching machine. These facilities are outside, or physically removed from, regular writing classrooms. When computers in regular classrooms are used for remediation, their presence suggests that the students who are assigned to them are, likewise, engaged in activities "outside" the main thrust of the classroom; the students are isolated, often labeled "slow."

The other myth fostered by instructor-centered teaching is the belief–and the anxiety–that the computer can replace the teacher. Deborah H. Holdstein and Tim Redman point out that the fear of automation may lead to defensive attitudes toward the computer as a competitor. This notion is patently false, as any writing instructor will realize who considers the complexity of the subject of writing, the need for individualization, and the difficulty in understanding written discourse. For others, including some misguided and misinformed administrators, automation offers the promise of teaching writing without employing teachers. They see it as a silver bullet in the fight against illiteracy, or as a way of cutting the budget for faculty salaries. They envision labs replacing expensive, low-enrollment, first- and second-year writing courses. Yet they underestimate the value of the students' previous education in writing, and they also ignore the complexity of the writing.

While the complexity of the writing is an important factor, an overemphasis on subject produces what Axelrod calls "subject-matter-oriented" teaching. In this mode, the subject, articulated in a book or a series of fixed lectures, is the focus of classroom activity, with teachers emphasizing writing as a skill, or set of skills. The goal is mastery of those skills: spelling, proofreading, mechanics, and so forth. When writing is reduced to a set of skills, however, one must acknowledge that computers might possibly perform those skills. Skill-oriented teaching leads to three myths regarding computers: that the word processor is merely a fancy typewriter, that spelling checkers impede learning of spelling, and that computerized style analysis will eliminate revision.

While the word processor is like a typewriter, it is a much more powerful tool.

Typewriters are useful for recording drafts of writing and for making texts more legible, but they do not affect writing in the way word processors do. The research of Bridwell, Geoffrey Sirc, and Robert Brooke shows us that word processors actually alter the cognitive processes by which writers compose and revise. Another researcher, Cheryl Geisler, explains how computers influence the nature of texts, their interpretation, and writers' perception of rhetorical situations. Thus the potential of the computer in the classroom appears to be much greater than that of a typewriter.

The potential for spelling and style programs is also greater than one would expect if one views them as substitutes or crutches that impede the learning of proofreading and revision skills. Contrary to the belief of some educators, spelling checkers do not automatically correct a student's misspelled words; they simply mark words that do not match the dictionary and allow the student to look up the words. Many writers say that spelling checkers improve spelling because they encourage students to use the dictionary. Style analyzers, such as the *Writer's Workbench*, as Daiute points out, were intended not to take over revision skills but to strengthen them (*Writing*). Besides, the *Writer's Workbench*, and other style-analysis programs, usually operate on the surface, dictional level of a document. Their commentary and suggestions only supplement the analysis a writer needs to do when revising. As we shall see, the misconception that style-analysis programs will take over revision may blind us to the productive use of these programs in the classroom.

Besides limiting our view of the usefulness of computers in the ways we have described, a subject-matter orientation may lead to an even more insidious misuse of the computer: a tendency on the part of teachers to introduce gender bias in computer instruction. It has become quite clear to educators over the last few years that boys are encouraged to excel in some subjects, while girls are not. Such gender bias tends to show up in science and math, where boys consistently score better than girls, partly because of teacher expectation. Those who see the computer as primarily a science or math tool, which it originally was but no longer is, may unconsciously encourage boys more than girls to work with the word processor, as more fitting to their scientific orientation. Gender bias is beginning to be noticed among commentators on computers and writing (Marcus, "Real-Time"). To the extent that writing teachers carry over this bias to word processing, we risk denying access to all students.

An overemphasis, then, on either the teacher or the subject in a writing class – at the expense of the third element, the student – may lead to narrow thinking about the computer's role. It may foster myths about the level, extent, and nature of computer use. The perception of computers as ancillary to our main purposes may do more harm than good. Fortunately, significant research developments in the writing process, as we shall presently see, have brought about changes in the way we view the instructional context and the role we and our students play in it. These changes will have an impact on how we view computers in the classroom.

Changes in Attitudes toward Classroom Teaching

The work of researchers in the processes of writing has allowed us to focus on the steps writers take in creating text: prewriting, drafting, rewriting, revising, proofreading. This shift in focus from earlier product-oriented approaches in subject matter has likewise altered the way we view the instructional context. I have space here for only a brief listing of some of the changes that have occurred. They include increased emphasis on the following:

1. collaborative writing, or shared authorship among students
2. the role of the teacher as co-writer, consultant, and reader rather than just evaluator
3. transactional, or "workplace," writing
4. peer editing and evaluation
5. group activities
6. the planning and drafting stages of writing

No doubt any writing teacher could add to this list of developments, which reflect the tendency to decentralize the classroom and to distribute the responsibility for learning among the teachers and students. The new emphases alter a number of instructional variables. For the sake of convenience, I would like to return to what Bridwell and Beach identify as three important factors in classroom teaching: teacher training, teachers' attitudes, and teachers' and students' roles (309–14). Examining these variables will allow us to clarify how the computer may cause us to rethink the larger issues surrounding the instructional context.

Computers and Teacher Training

As Bridwell and Beach and others illustrate, the kinds of pre- and in-service training that teachers receive help determine their performance in the classroom and that of their students. Joyce Carroll's work indicates, for example, that the more process-oriented the project is, the better the teacher learns to interact with students during various stages of writing. We may assume, then, that teacher training in general – whether in writing processes, audience awareness, or computer use – carries over into classroom practice. Training in computer use is particularly important now because our profession is in a transition phase from pen-and-pencil composition to word processing, and from traditional educational methods to computer-assisted instruction.

What is the nature of training in computer use among writing teachers, and how does it occur? For most writing teachers there are two types of training: training in using word processing and training in using computer-assisted instruction. Such training may come from a number of sources: graduate courses (offered by English or education departments), seminars (offered either through departments or school districts), private firms (either retail outlets or hardware companies), and organizations (NCTE, CCCC, etc.). Books are also available, such as a 1986 publication of NCTE called *Write It Yourself: CAI for the Composition Classroom* (Selfe). For many writing teachers, however, the training comes hard won through trial and error, and the lack of training may slow down the transition to word processing.

There has been little systematic research into the effect of teacher training on computer use, although a number of researchers point out its importance (Selfe, "Dancing"; Barker, "Issues"; Rodrigues and Rodrigues). Woodruff et al. note that the teachers in their study of the use of word processors by eighth-grade writers had extensive experience with computers in general and with word processors in particular. Marcus, in *Practical Writing Resource Kit*, points out that students gain the most benefit when there is "a major commitment from the instructor" (7), but most teachers I know are unwilling to become actively involved in word processing without feeling that they are well prepared.

Well-prepared teachers can make a significant difference in the success of computer use. Rodrigues and Rodrigues emphasize that writing teachers should be comfortable with the tool, in order to avoid presenting it to students as just a fancy typewriter. In addition, familiarity with the word processor, they note, allows teachers to maintain the focus on writing, rather than on the skills of word processing, and to anticipate some of the changes that word processing will make in classroom activities. We might add that training in computer-assisted instruction will enable teachers to show students how to interpret computer feedback from style-analysis programs intelligently.

Computers and Teachers' Attitudes

Just as we saw earlier that there is no consensus as to what teaching style is most effective, so there is no one attitude among writing teachers that works best to create a productive environment for computers. Although we might expect that a sort of guarded enthusiasm toward computers would lead to their productive use in teaching, we have no guarantee of this. We do, however, have evidence that teachers' attitudes toward writing affect their perceptions about the quality of their students' work.

In their discussion of the instructional context, Bridwell and Beach shed light on the relationship between attitudes about appropriate style for academic writing and teachers' evaluation of student writing. They discuss research showing that attitudes do make a difference and that, for example, teachers make assumptions about "appropriate" school writing that guide their assessments (311–13). Some teachers, it was discovered, consider a personal, assertive, opinionated tone inappropriate for first-year college writing. Moreover, according to Bridwell and Beach, the literature indicates that our teaching methods may depend on our attitudes toward writing instruction: some teachers value a variety of writing genres; others value specific elements of syntax, usage, and organization. As Carole McAllister has suggested, there may be a relationship between teachers' attitudes toward computer use and their perception of the quality of students' writing (37). These explorations of teachers' attitudes lead one to ask whether it is possible that certain attitudes about computers determine the effectiveness of their use as writing tools.

What are some common attitudes toward computers in the classroom among writing teachers? One does not have to look far in the literature to uncover opinions about computers; evidence of the range of attitudes from skepticism to enthusiasm abounds. But nowhere are these attitudes more clearly presented than in the Spring 1983 issue of *Focus*, a journal on teaching language arts. This issue, which is still available from NCTE, contains a number of articles testifying to the mixture of trepidation and hope with which most English teachers first approached the computer. Here are some examples of the titles: "Getting on the Computer Bandwagon," "Two-Point-Five Cheers: The Computers Are Coming," "Overcoming Computer Anxiety with Word Processing," and "Computers and the Obsolete English Teacher."

These articles represent the ambivalence of a profession that found itself in a state of change. Some writers explore both the advantages and disadvantages of the computer (Stephenson). Others – almost all – note the suspicion and cautiousness among their colleagues (Hunter; Selfe, "Dancing"; Rollins). Machine anxiety, the phobia toward nonhumanistic devices, occupies the focus of some of the articles (Selfe, "Dancing"; Appleby). Other writers point out the uncertainty facing computer users in English (Marling; Jobst; Appleby). What these articles in their totality reflect, as I noted, are the curiously ambivalent attitudes surrounding the transition to computers in the English classroom.

By saying "the" transition, I do not mean to belie the variety of experiences English departments had in adjusting to computers. But there are a few generalizations one might risk in this regard. That transition had some special characteristics that shaped the attitudes of teachers, as reflected in the 1983 issue of *Focus*. First, in many cases, computers "fell out of the sky" – which is to say they were mandated from administrators or forward-thinking deans and chairpersons. They were not usually requested by instructors; consequently, for many teachers the first computer was seen as an imposition. Second, the transition was not driven by research in classroom applications. In fact, the early days of computer use were haphazard; at one time I received a grant to study software only to find that there was no software to study. During those days few people were experienced in using word processors even though they could vaguely see their instructional value. Third, the transition period of 1983–84 saw instructors almost polarized as either skeptical or effusive, two attitudes that could not last, that needed to be tempered with sound experience.

I contend that this situation – the imposition of computers on teachers without adequate research into their needs – influenced the attitudes of instructors in 1983. And those attitudes may continue to shape our realities. Today we see our actual practice of using computers in classrooms shifting: where, previously, the emphasis was on the computer as teacher, lately we see the computer being used more as a tool. Software development is becoming more sophisticated, and research in word processing and writing is beginning to take identifiable directions (Barker, "Studies"; Hawisher, "Research in Word Processing"; Haring-Smith). But the skepticism remains. While we now know more about how to use computers, it may be even harder for the machines to earn their way into our classrooms and labs because we require more specific applications and we demand increased instructional productivity. The informed skepticism of today reflects our growing experience with computers, and it parallels our development in the third, and perhaps most important, area of classroom trends, the role of the teacher.

Computers and Teachers' and Students' Roles

According to Kenneth Kantor and others, the traditional role of the English teacher has followed an authoritative model. The teacher, in this model, controlled the class, assigned tasks, and evaluated performance. Certainly these functions were and are important and mirror the instructional context in other disciplines. As I pointed out earlier, however, research into the nature of writing since the early 1980s has given us reason to reconsider whether this model is appropriate for writing instruction. In fact, this model may present some significant limitations to writing instruction.

In particular, those limitations center on the role of the teacher and, at the same time, the role of the student. One limitation is that the authoritative model confines the interaction of the teacher and student to one relationship, instead of allowing a range of relationships, some of which might nurture the student's self-perception as a writer. Second, this model fosters a skewed vision of the writing process because it emphasizes the audience as evaluator, rather than the audience as someone who seeks certain information. The current interest in transactional writing suggests that we should help students focus on what their audience needs to know, rather than on what their audience will criticize. Finally, the authoritative model emphasizes the product of writing rather than the process of writing. We find that students benefit more from examining how they go about writing than from sweating out how error-free they can make their papers. It stands to reason, then, that a less error-oriented approach would work with students, that we might concentrate on helping them design and revise rather than correct. We might start collaborating with them instead of judging them.

Collaboration entails rethinking the role of the teacher, and in this area the computer seems to have a significant impact. Research is showing us that collaboration using computers occurs in two areas: teachers collaborating with students and students collaborating with each other. Andrea Herrmann, as she describes in a case study of collaborative poetry writing in her elementary classroom, observed students beginning to define ways to interact with each other while writing (they were encouraged by the teacher and facilitated by the highly visible computer screen containing their work). She speculates that the ability to collaborate is "closely linked to an individual's self-esteem" ("Interim Report" 171).

It appears that collaboration occurs among students from different "tracks" (gifted, developmental, and so on) and different socioeconomic levels. Other researchers note a similar mixing, or leveling effect, among collaborators at the computer (Selfe and Wahlstrom; Bernhardt and Appleby). Students who share the writing task, either among themselves or with their teacher, alter their behavior in ways that suggest significant new directions for the instructional context.

It is important to recognize just how the computer enhances collaboration and process-oriented teaching in general. Of course, much of the result of word processing depends on the kind of computer and the complexity of the system used. Nevertheless, we can make some observations about the computer's effect. On a very simple level, computer screens differ from sheets of paper because they are more visible: the letters and words are clearer to read, and the screen can be viewed by more than one person *as the writing occurs.* Anyone who has taught in a computerized classroom knows how easy it is to engage students in discussions about what they are writing, because their work is prominently displayed on the screens. But researchers are discovering even more elaborate changes effected by computers and writing. Selfe surveyed students and discovered that the word processors seemed to motivate intense collaboration among writers in computer labs. Moreover, she identified several other results: greater "effort sharing"– a mutual awareness of writing problems among writers; patterns of how people share information about computers; and altered methods of revising based on the more "public" nature of computerized writing ("Creating").

But perhaps even more important, writing with a word processor encourages a more flexible mode of composing than does writing with pen and paper. Students can easily move from one point to another in an ongoing composition; they can move around, writing where their thought processes take them instead of going from beginning to end of a composition. Using a computer challenges their inventiveness and ability to plan, whether they are writing journals or essays, or building systems of files. In fact, studies indicate that word processors affect composing behavior in at least two important ways: in the amount of writing produced and in the composing patterns that produce writing (Barker, "Studies" 119).

If teachers are to benefit from the more egalitarian effect of computers in the classroom, they must rethink some important assumptions about their role. They may coach, referee, and manage more, while at the same time they may evaluate, judge, and correct less. I, for one, welcome such changes, partly because I have never seen myself as a stereotyped English teacher and I have always regretted the images of schoolmarms and wimps that that stereotype evokes. Using computers in my teaching has helped dispel negative attitudes among students toward English teachers. For their part, teachers in the new classroom may see the computer conference become, if not the primary, certainly a more important mode of interaction with students. We may need, finally, to study ways to encourage group writing with computers, computer communications and publications, and computerized writers' networks.

The Glass Canvas: Classroom 2000

I have seen and read about a number of versions of the future of classroom teaching; some are video-computer arcades, with the teacher at the center, wizardlike, omnipotent. Others, even Joseph Axelrod's tamer version, were chock full of instructional technology and short on teachers. Consideration of the impact of computers on writing seems to evoke speculation about the future. I would like to review some trends that indicate how computers may be involved in the evolution of classroom teaching of writing.

One such trend is the increasing externalization of our thought processes as a result of computers. Derek A. Kelly observed, in *Documenting Computer Application Systems*, that, "[i]n a manner of speaking, a computer is a model of part of the mind" (139). What he means, I think, is that computers mirror the mind because they externalize our cognitive processes. What was once the hidden process of mentally rearranging information becomes visible in our word processors. But this observation raises some challenging questions. What do we know about the mind and brain? How does the computer go about externalizing? And, finally, how does externalization tie in with writing instruction?

One way computer programs make our thinking external is to reveal the choices that writers make. We see this revelation in keystroke programs, which – much like the protocol studies of Swarts, Flower, and Hayes – record and time a writer's fingers as they press on the keys. This information is stored and may be reviewed by the writer or the researcher. The programs, such as those developed at the University of Minnesota, are valuable research tools, allowing us to peer into composing behavior in a new way, as if we were seeing writing from the inside out. Perhaps most important, the programs enable us to examine how extensively writers revise using computers, and to assess the relation between the amount of revision and its quality.

But keystroke programs are not used just in the research lab. In fact, they are making their way into the hands of composition teachers. I reviewed an article for *Computers and Composition* in which a writing teacher described not only how a keystroke program was designed but how it was used by students and teachers, in group activities, as a way of helping writers perceive their dictional and other compositional choices. The author argued that the presence of such data about composing skills and strategies offers students and teachers a wholly new ground on which to approach writing.

The computer has become a communications device both in revealing the nature of our writing processes and in enabling us to cooperate on our endeavors. By displaying our writing, making drafts public, the computer discloses the successive stages in the generation of documents. We are painters on a glass canvas, visible to our subjects and our peers. We have traded off the privilege of concealing the unfinished. In composition classrooms, students and teachers may share files and documents, collaborating both in composing and in deriving standards for student writing. An approach of this sort follows the theoretical guidelines in such works as Karen LeFevre's *Invention as a Social Act*. By using mail facilities in networked classrooms, students participate in computer-based discussions; in the process, they not only learn to communicate more clearly in writing but have an opportunity to share their inventive techniques.

The computer also has a way of making our teaching more explicit; it can make us more open to our students and ourselves, without compromising our professionalism. The techniques of collaboration with students, and the revolutionary stance toward the teacher's authority, allow students to witness pedagogical strategies, to catch the magician putting the rabbit into the hat. Just as we talk of a "self-effacing" computer program – one that so mirrors the human mind as to require no instructions or tutoring – so we may begin to see classroom teaching as becoming self-effacing in a verbal as well as a physical sense. One instructor I know merely sits at the computer and composes, allowing students to observe his progress, become involved, and ask questions as they need to. He reported to me that students will often get into heated discussions about his composing without his having to challenge them. In our lab at Texas Tech University we use a transparent monitor: a liquid crystal screen attached to a personal computer and displayed with an overhead projector. Such a device, well used, offers an opportunity to display the writing process in ways not previously available.

I am reminded of a conversation I had with a colleague from the University of Minnesota on the subject of the changing role of the writing teacher in the computer age. She suggested that teachers might become "education managers," responding to students as their needs arose. Most teachers now think that they determine the content of classroom or course subject matter. One teacher might emphasize the analytical approach to style, while another might consider teaching style as a matter of practice and imitation. In both cases, the teacher determines the content. But imagine teaching in a classroom that uses computers so accurately as to mirror real-life situations, with audience parameters, data archives, form models, analytical tools, and graphic instruments. In such a classroom, students might learn experientially. They might recognize gaps in their knowledge and consult their coach-teacher. The coach-teacher might direct them to information, but might also assign learning exercises designed to strengthen skills. In this way the relationship between teacher, student, and the real world becomes more fluid, the applications of theory to practice more clearly defined than at present.

Such developments will undoubtedly result from more profound influences than the computer, which seems more and more like a part of educational change than the cause of the change. In this article I have tried to show how the nature of our thinking about the writing classroom is evolving, and how computers are part of that evolution. In the way that we train ourselves, recognize and adapt our attitudes, and conceive of our roles as teachers we incorporate technology into our classroom and open our classroom to innovative approaches.

Ethical Considerations of Educational Computer Use

Helen J. Schwartz

———◆———

Although a new technology may in itself be value-free, its use can never be free of implicit values and the need for ethical consideration. Therefore, as we use computers in education, particularly in writing instruction, we should ask a number of questions. How does the medium affect the relation between students and teacher, as well as the students' rights to honest treatment, to original thought, and to ownership of ideas within an intellectual community? Ethical issues arise, too, when we consider the distribution of software and hardware: How will software be produced and made available to schools and individuals so that the users get good value and producers get a fair return for intellectual property? As a new generation of teachers is being trained, under what conditions will they learn about computer use? And what values will determine the distribution of hardware?

As a teacher using computers, a designer of computer-assisted instruction, and a citizen, I'd like to share my views with an audience concerned with educational use of computers: teachers who use computers, designers and vendors who produce software and hardware, administrators who plan and budget for computer use in education, government officials who set policy and priorities for support to education. In speaking to this audience, I will discuss three different areas that raise ethical considerations: the design and classroom use of software, the funding and distribution of software, and access to computers.

The Design and Use of Software

The lecture-discussion format of most classrooms represents a solution to an economic problem: how the most material can be conveyed to a number of students by one teacher (Leonard 48–50). The speed and capability of computers seems to offer an educational dream of endlessly patient, individually prescribed instructional modules delivered at the student's convenience. Going beyond the tedium of early drill and practice, new programs – whether they are computer-assisted instruction (CAI) or applications for utility programs such as word processing and databases – reflect an increased sophistication in software development and educational practice. But the inherent inflexibility of the computer must be recognized and subordinated to the educational goals set by teachers.

Responsible use of software first requires evaluation and integration into classroom practice to ensure that the design of software does not dictate the ethical relation between teachers and students. Teachers adapt to different students and their moods almost unconsciously, but because of the student-faculty ratio and the organization of the classroom, they cannot be as effective as a tutor with an individual. Software can help students work individually (or in groups), but the teacher must take into account the fact that the software's structure is inflexible and may not be suitable to a student's learning style. The questions to ask before buying software are these: Can the software be used so as to preserve the responsibilities of teachers to students and of students to their own learning? Is the software designed to respect the student's ownership of ideas and work? Does it deal honestly with students? Does it respect the individuality of the user – her style of learning, his right to think originally, idiosyncratically, or playfully?

Responsibilities of Teachers and Students

Responsibility is based on ability and freedom of choice. Teachers have the responsibility to guide students toward improvement; students have the responsibility to take action and accept the consequences. The popular image of computers "force-feeding" learning into passive students not only is unrealistic but makes teachers less accountable to students and students less accountable for their own learning. It is important to remember this because computers can function excellently as enforcers and controllers. We don't call them that, of course. Instead we read advertising about the wonders of "computer-managed instruction." The computer can keep track of how well a student scores, which mistakes she makes, which errors he repeats, what programs have been assigned, and which modules completed. I'm not against this convenience; I only caution that we should be sure that computers are used with the needs and abilities of students in mind.

For example, three kinds of programs exist for error correction (not including spelling checkers): (1) CAI for drill; (2) delivery packages in which a reviewer identifies writing problems in a student-generated textfile (usually with drill or an on-line handbook available for instruction); and (3) software that finds and diagnoses problems in student-generated textfiles. With drill, if students do not improve their scores, does the fault lie with the student, the program, or the instructional setting? Will students who master the computer program be able to incorporate their learning in their own writing – or have they simply learned to guess well in a limited field (the sentence presented by the computer drill for consideration), rather than to revise their internal model and rules for what is correct? The responsibility of teachers to students is not over once the program has been selected; they owe their students continual monitoring of computer effectiveness.

With teacher feedback on student-generated text, what are the issues of responsibility? Current thinking suggests that teachers should not mark every error but should focus on one kind of error and have the student work on a cluster of similar mistakes in the paper (Hartwell and Bentley). A program such as *Prose* allows a teacher to insert in a student's textfile several comments (which can be linked to an online handbook, examples, and drill). The teacher can then set the order in which the student sees the comments along with the chance to revise the textfile for correctness. In this way the teacher can create an individual tutorial from a student's own work. In contrast, error-detecting programs under development, such as *Critique* and *Mina* (see Hull et al.), identify all errors, often in an overwhelming array. If the student does not "improve" after using the software, whose fault is it? There is a tendency with computers to attribute infallibility to the technology, but the ethical use of computers keeps the issue of responsibility between student and teacher as the central concern.

The question also arises with software over control of the learning environment. Do students have enough freedom in using a program so that they can take responsibility for their own learning? Let's look first at a case in which this issue emerges – in the relatively rule-bound learning of grammar. We can design drill-and-practice programs that diagnose a student's errors and vary the number and level of difficulty of questions on that basis. Since such programs can be complex, we might be tempted to build in a mechanism that routes students automatically to the modules they need. That is, with the best intentions in the world, we would have started using computers to control.

But what happens in such cases? First, students may spend their time and energy in resisting the system and trying to subvert it. Second, we give up the "peripheral," backdoor possibilities of learning. Have you ever watched someone learning to play *PacMan* or another video game? The rules are fairly complex, yet no directions are given on the machine. How do people learn? They watch others, and they experiment themselves. They set their own level of difficulty. How does this apply to our grammar-program example? We need to accept the implications of our ignorance about learning. Since we can't be sure how various students will learn, why shouldn't students try modules that are too hard for them? They may learn something, or they may at worst waste a few minutes finding out that the prescribed module and level are more suitable.

When we turn to the more complex, less rule-governed case of the writing process, we can see the same issue of student freedom and responsibility for learning. Investigation of how writers actually compose reveals that people vary widely among themselves and from one assignment to another (Bridwell, Johnson, and Brehe). In something as complex as the writing process, therefore, no program should prescribe one method as *the* method. A relatively inflexible program such as *Writing Is Thinking*, even though the model is theoretically sound, enforces one process. In contrast, with invention software, a number of programs provide a choice of tutorials. For example, William Wresch's *Writer's Helper* provides assistance in finding a topic, developing ideas, organizing them, and checking the resulting draft for certain stylistic and organizational features. Schwartz and Nachman's *Organize* allows users to choose modules on development, audience analysis, argumentation, and approaches (such as outlining and freewriting). *HBJ Writer* also maintains freedom with its combination of prewriting aids (freewriting, nutshelling, planning – for argumentation and outlining – and invisible writing), word processor, and revision aids (such as a spelling and homonym checker, feedback on stylistic features and punctuation). The teacher is not put in the position – by the software design – of presenting a single model that can be used in only one way. And although a teacher may assign a particular prewriting or revising module in such software, the student has access to the others.

Student Ownership of Texts

Teachers should also respect students' ownership of their work. Local area networks (LAN) make it possible for the teacher to call up any student's text for teacher review or for peer review. To ensure that students retain ownership of their work, the teacher should be certain either that the system prevents the teacher – or another student – from calling up a student's text without permission or that an agreed-upon etiquette gives students control of their work. Whether with LANs or stand-alone personal computers, students who write on the word processor should not have to turn in every draft. Cynthia Selfe and Billie Wahlstrom, in "An Emerging Rhetoric of Collaboration," report that students develop protocol and strategies for keeping their work private, even in a crowded computer lab: by turning down the brightness or scrolling the text off the screen when someone stops to talk. When students own their texts, it is their right to control access by others.

Communication by computer creates for students a setting similar to that of publishing academics. The individual retains control over his or her work, but an exchange of efforts fostered by the computer encourages responsible "publication" and response to the work of others. The idea of a community of scholars becomes real in a local setting. Recent theory by Kenneth Bruffee, as described in "Collaborative Learning," as well as Hillocks's meta-analysis of research findings in "What Works in Teaching Composition," stresses the value and effectiveness of collaborative learning. Students who discover ideas and form through problem solving and group work are able to master information in a realistic context, while peer support can provide a testing ground and environment for change. In such a setting, students can engage in argument and debate, in comparison to a set exercise, say, to explicate a poem or define Machiavellianism. For example, with Schwartz's *Seen*, students can develop their ideas through an open-ended tutorial (for instance, on character analysis or essay interpretation); feedback is provided by peers who share ideas on a bulletin board included as part of the program.

The computer can make collaboration more convenient because it does not require that all students be in the same place simultaneously or that multiple copies be made. Students can collaborate when they have access to shared textfiles or program output. Instead of being a medium to alienate one person from another, the computer can bring together those who otherwise feel isolated from their peers. The architecture, seating arrangement, and teaching style of the traditional classroom ensure communication between the teacher and the student as a dyad, but work shared by means of the computer builds a sense of community, whether the means is a specific program such as *HBJ Writer*'s provision for peer review or *Seen*'s bulletin board, access to word-processed journals stored on a hard disk, or some kind of systemwide bulletin board. At Gallaudet, Trent Batson's deaf students sit in a circle, each at a computer, and use the ENFI system (English Natural Form Instruction) to communicate in writing, seeing the ongoing dialogue at the top of the screen as they compose their own message on the bottom. Jerome Woolpy describes how students at Earlham use the structure of the *Delphi* system to ask and answer questions in a genetics course and then receive comment and evaluation from the instructor or advanced students. This is more than a pedagogical method; it is an important medium for achieving responsible and responsive individuality in a community of scholars.

Honesty to the User

Another ethical consideration in software design involves the way the program treats the student. Responses should be honest and humane – a harder task than it looks. A teacher decides when to use praise to encourage a student for partial achievement and when to use criticism to spur greater efforts. A teacher's imitation of the wrath of God, delivered with a twinkle in the eye, may be appropriate to the situation and well received. But a software designer must write a response that will be not only accurate (as discussed below) but rhetorically appropriate and motivating to the student.

It is hard to find responses in CAI that are both honest and humane, especially if they are generated at random (for variety) or without the ability to evaluate or even understand the semantic content of a student's response. "Tremendous, Helen!" loses its impact when my response was "I can't think of anything to say." Students soon learn to distrust facile praise.

Other kinds of computer feedback, like statistics in style checkers, may be useless or misleading to the unsophisticated writer. For example, the *Homer* program (Lanham and Cohen) can map the writer's use of nominalizations – in this case, words ending in *-tion*. Furthermore, the program delivers statistics (e.g., 12 out of 189 words in a written passage were *-tion* words) and evaluation, such as "Do you need all those 'SHUN' words? Some might become verbs – experiment!!" For skilled writers, this feedback might be sufficient. They would know that *tuition* shouldn't be changed to a verb. They might even notice that the word *enrollment* hadn't been counted as a nominalization, so their score was really "worse" than *Homer* said. Or they might realize that a letter from the provost to the faculty about enrollment trends would naturally be likely to have more nominalizations than an essay on "the best teacher I ever had." However, for a writer barely staying on that bucking maverick called written English, the warning about *-tion* words may seem useless. Worse yet, students may feel that if only they can get a "score" within the acceptable range, their essays will be substantively better. Such writing to a formula can promote a magical view of revision and undermine a student's growth in self-judgment for rewriting. The computer's responses should be appropriate to the student's mastery of the subject and encourage the responsibility for text that comes with ownership.

A teacher can help a student evaluate and use the program's output. Teachers and user manuals should make the point clearly that the surface revision addressed by style checkers will probably not substantively improve a paper. Tinkering to meet a statistical norm will not lead to good writing.

We get into a more difficult problem when we deal with programs that do attempt to give substantive feedback on critical thinking. Can you imagine a multiple-choice question on the theme of *Huckleberry Finn*? Actually, that's not a bad approach if each answer is acceptable and will branch to a different tutorial.

But what if the program calls for free-form responses? Sometimes the program's attempt to respond to meaning (although the program cannot understand the student's semantic intent) can be amusing, once the student catches on. For example, students using an invention program discovered that the computer responded to unforeseen questions by saying, "Yes, that's OK." These students were soon getting computer printouts in which they asked, "Is premarital sex permissible?" (Burns, "Recollections" 29).

Another program prints a paragraph on the screen and asks the student to explain what motivates one character's actions. When I typed my answer, I focused on the character's feelings and did not mention the character's girlfriend. The response gently suggested that I hadn't got it quite right and urged me to answer again. As a PhD in English, I reacted to this response with a "Hrumph!" When I saw a bright non-English major run the program and get the same response, I was more upset; his answer seemed acceptable to me, yet he was told he was wrong and he believed the computer. I suspect the software is programmed to accept an answer that contains "key words" such as the name of the character's girlfriend. If so, then if I typed, "He was not motivated by Judy," the incorrect answer would be accepted; if I said, "He was upset because of the inattention of his inamorata," the correct answer would be rejected.

How useful a program would be that could truly understand and respond! But I don't foresee an accurate program for free-form entries in the near future. Until we can design programs that understand, then I am unwilling to use software that may give misleading answers – either by judging an acceptable answer as incorrect or by evaluating a wrong answer as correct. At times a teacher can make such mistakes, too, but humans have the option of reflection and recursion: I can bring up the matter again with students; they can question me.

A positive example of humane feedback comes from *Blue Pencil*, a drill-and-practice program designed by Robert Bator and Mitsuru Yamada. The program calls up a paragraph on screen, lists how many errors of a particular kind remain undetected, allows the student to correct the errors (with feedback and hints). The following comment appeared after one of the questions: "That was my toughest question." The beauty of this answer is that it acknowledges the achievement (or at least the daring) of students at different levels of mastery. A student who got the answer right after one try could feel justifiable pride; for students who never got it right, this response provides feedback for evaluating the test's difficulty.

Creativity through Play

So far I have focused on computer-assisted instruction (rather than utility programs such as word processing) to discuss values (responsibility, ownership, and honesty) that seem most noticeable in their absence. But playful creativity is a positive value I believe we should provide, whether with CAI or other programs.

I hope we will avoid using computers primarily to test students. I often hear people question the positive findings about computer use on the basis that computers are novel toys but their value will decrease when the novelty wears off. I've seen a few tutorials that made even the computer dull and tedious, but for the most part I remain intrigued with computer use. Let me be clear that I decided almost from the beginning that I would not play games on the computer. Aside from a brief fling with *Adventure*, I have remained true to my pledge – wiser, and no doubt duller, than the *PacMan* aficionados. Reports confirm my experience of the intrinsic fascination with a medium that takes one's ideas seriously and mirrors them for contemplation or manipulation (Turkle).

According to Johan Huizinga in *Homo Ludens*, play is a safe, rule-governed activity without serious consequences. I value the computer because it can provide a playground. A bulletin board can be a safe place to try out a pen-name-signed essay, whether that forum is a cork-filled rectangle on a classroom wall, in *Delphi* on a hard disk attached to networked computers, or within a CAI program such as *Seen*. A word-processing program can make revision playful, with its electronic text encouraging a tentativeness that keeps egos unbruised by criticism. A student can actually watch and hear how another person reads the text, gaining understanding about reader response on which to base a revision.

Teachers have a choice. They can use word processing as a glorified typewriter, or they can use the new medium for scholarly community, creativity, and discovery. With CAI, software developers and teachers have the responsibility to work together to create and use software that respects the individuality of students and treats them honestly and humanely. Teachers can take good software and make it punitive, or they can soften the inflexibility of CAI programs by recommending it to certain students and, within a context, explaining its limitations. As with textbooks, teachers and instructional designers must each do their jobs well.

The Funding and Distribution of Software

According to the president of Carnegie Mellon University, Richard M. Cyert, "the greatest obstacle to achieving an educational impact [with computers] is the need to create new software" (4). However, the production of high-quality software depends on how it is funded and distributed.

Ethical issues arise concerning the distribution of software, because of the ease in copying. Educators want high-quality, reliable software; authors and publishers want a fair return for their investment and work. The copyright law provides safeguards for intellectual property, but because technology is making it easier to reproduce intellectual property (from books, tapes, and software), protection for such products cannot rely on enforcement of the law but rather on a widespread acceptance of fairness: workers are worthy of their hire.

The Production of High-Quality Software

Good software requires effective pedagogical design, programming skill, and reliable testing. Although one person may be able to write a book (and even produce it now, with desktop publishing), few individuals have the skills required to produce good software all by themselves. Producing high-quality software more often requires a team and a great deal of time (see Selfe, *Computer-Assisted Instruction*).

If the participants in software development deserve reward, where will the compensation come from? Academics who author software programs often report that they get little professional credit toward renewal, tenure, or promotion. (However, the reliable review of software by organizations such as EDUCOM or through state initiatives, as in Minnesota, may improve this situation, resulting in financial and professional credibility.) University funding provides time and facilities, as do some grants (although grants for software have become more rare in recent years). When universities get in the business of selling software – as was the case with the University of California, Los Angeles, and *HBJ Writer* – the lion's share may go to the university, even though development costs have been borne primarily by grant funds. Some hardware vendors support software development (though usually after the fact) if only by featuring software at their convention displays. They know that no one wants hardware unless suitable software exists. And as colleges buy hardware, they demand software as an adjunct to book purchases; therefore, publishers are now beginning to buy software outright or under a contract similar to a textbook agreement. Finally, new distribution schemes – through software consortia or shareware – offer low-cost software to the buyer and a reasonable return per sale to the author.

Teachers should be able to modify software for their students' needs, just as they now supplement textbooks with dittoed materials. Increasingly, software supports such revision or teachers learn to use template textfiles to guide students (see Rodrigues and Rodrigues). Nevertheless, I believe there will always be a demand for new commercial software, produced with careful control of quality, but at great cost. At present, as the quality and cost of production increase, new partnerships between area specialists, producers, and distributors must be developed. Just as textbooks are written by teachers in diverse institutions for different student populations, so too must new arrangements be found so that all software is not developed by publishers alone or only by large research institutions.

However, if distributors cannot get a fair return for making such software available, then educators will not get high-quality programs. The possibility of piracy casts a long shadow over such market considerations.

The Problem of Piracy

Software is more or less easily copyable. A court decision has ruled that buyers are entitled to make one backup copy for their personal use if the software package does not provide one. As long as software is marketed without a copy protection mechanism, individuals with a little skill in computer use can make as many copies as they want, for only the cost of the blank disks. As new ways to prevent copying come on the market, they are often followed by copying devices to break the protection schemes. Copy protection raises the cost of producing software, lowers its reliability, and takes up disk space that might be used for additional functions in a program.

If consumers routinely make multiple copies, what protects the producers' interests? How will producers and authors make a profit that encourages further development of good software? Some publishers have responded to widespread piracy by keeping prices steep. Sales volume may be low, but with a high return per program, producers can recover costs and make a profit. This strategy, however, ignores the budget limitations of educational and home users. And a policy based on the assumption that people will make unauthorized copies of a program may seem to legitimize or encourage such behavior.

Users sometimes rationalize piracy as an alternative to a reasonable examination policy. Some companies have encouraged people to share software with others, who, if satisfied, voluntarily send in payment, often receiving the manual in return. With *PC-Write*, for example, if a user gets a copy from a friend, he or she is encouraged to register it (for $75) because the company will send $25 for any person who subsequently copies and registers the software from this registered copy. However, returns to the producers of such "shareware" have varied, with the greatest return going to programs that require complex manuals.

To date, excellent programs have often been available only from the author or from small companies. With this method of distribution, the only ways to preview are by attending demonstrations or by reading descriptions in journals. Some reviews have appeared in computer journals such as *InfoWorld* or machine-specific magazines like *MacUser*. Computer-related writing journals such as *Computers and Composition* or *Research in Word Processing Newsletter* regularly publish reviews specifically of writing software. However, the need to examine before buying cannot be adequately met until software reviews appear in easily accessible and reliable publications (including the most widely read journals in the field, such as *College English, College Composition and Communication*, and *English Journal*). Furthermore, demonstration copies must be routinely available, and return policies or buying-on-approval practices must conform to the procedures for review and payment that prevail in schools. Such policies, however, require the resources of big publishers.

There is no ethical justification for piracy, whether for personal use or for resale. Copying is justified only when the company does not provide a backup and the buyer makes one copy, as provided by law, but does not use it as a second functioning program.

Who Will Pay for High-Quality Software?

If users do not pirate computer programs, how can consumers obtain quality software? Either education must do without this resource, prices must come down, or new strategies for development must be devised.

As the market for software grows, publishers have been seeking innovative ways to meet the needs of educators. First, as the installed base of computers has increased, competition has been lowering the price of software, since a small profit at large volume can produce acceptable income. Low prices, in turn, make it possible to sell software directly to individual students, rather than to a school. Some software is being packaged with books, or publishers provide software free with a certain minimum adoption of a text. In effect, this practice passes along the costs of software to the student and pays royalties to the software's author.

Some schemes depend on an ethic of nonpiracy. Much commercial software is dropping prices as well as copy protection, relying on fair use by home or business consumers. (The reason for such apparent trust may actually be the prevalence of computers with hard disks that require unprotected software for easy loading into the machine.) In other cases, software is copyable, but a noncopyable startup disk is required in order to "boot" the program or must be inserted every two weeks to show that the original disk is still around. Such a scheme may work to prevent piracy in an office with occasional users scattered throughout a large office, but its effectiveness in a school lab must depend on an ethic of nonpiracy among faculty and students. The notion of copying software as an intellectual pastime or indoor sport must evolve into an ethic of respect for ownership of intellectual property.

Another approach is to expect the institution to assume the costs of software. The sale of lab packs gives the school one program per computer at a reasonable cost, and also the responsibility of protecting the software from copying. Finally, site licenses sell a facility the right to produce multiple copies. So, for example, a university can buy a site license for a program and either make copies available in clusters or sell copies to the students (for further strategies, see Arms). For such approaches to be fair to both sides, schools and universities must include reasonable budgets for software as a routine, expected item in their overall costs.

Another way of providing inexpensive software is to shift the burden of purchase from either the student or the institution to the government. In California, for example, the state has made available as public-domain software a word-processing program (*Fredwriter*) and a database program (*Data Relator*) – copyable but not for sale. The state is also reviewing software and distributing one copy of recommended software to each school. Minnesota, too, as we noted, has developed a statewide program for review of software. Furthermore, the Minnesota Educational Computing Consortium (MECC) has been producing software and is now marketing it to school systems.

New answers are evolving. It seems clear to me that prices must come down, but also that consumers (whether individuals, schools, or government boards) must adhere to a social contract of responsible use and payment if software is to develop with quality and reliability. Just as we teach students to respect the intellectual property of writers through citations, we need to convey the idea that individuals or groups who invest creativity and effort in software development are entitled to the same respect and protection.

Access to Computers

If we are to believe recent ads for computers, any parent or school board that does not provide students with access to computers is dooming the little victims to lifelong unemployment and intellectual underdevelopment.

Is it necessary to have access to computers? No. Is it desirable? Yes – assuming that suitable software exists and trained teachers can integrate it effectively and humanely into their classrooms. The question then becomes when and how to introduce computer use.

Although CAI is often easy to use, more complex programs take some time to master – for example, databases, word processors, and graphics packages. Once people are familiar with programs, they can often pick up (or refamiliarize themselves with) a program quickly, but an initial investment of time is required for learning a program's concept as well as the syntax and procedures of its operation. The power of computers in intellectual and economic application will increasingly allow the integration of information – finding, sorting, combining, analyzing, modifying, and, finally, communicating it. These procedures are not new, but the functioning of the equipment is. Consider the skills I need to do the following activities (all possible with existing software): I do a computer search of the literature on a topic, get machine-readable copies of selected items, then "mark" selected passages that I keep in a database for retrieval into a text I write. I use a spreadsheet to try different "what-if" scenarios with data, projecting trends for five, ten, and twenty years; then I represent those trends graphically and integrate them into my text. When I have a draft ready, I share it with selected colleagues by electronic mail or on a computer-based bulletin board of colleagues. When I have revised my article, I submit it electronically or on disk to a potential publisher.

Anyone can learn to perform these operations, but the process is a long and cumulative one. Educators generally agree that such training should occur within classes in a discipline rather than as part of special computer literacy instruction (National Task Force 61); writing classes are often seen as an equitable place to introduce computer use, since so many students take the courses, regardless of race, gender, or academic major. However, many teachers fear that the time required for training leads to a decrease in subject-matter learning.

I don't know when the nuts-and-bolts skills should be taught, but I suspect that it is best to teach skills such as typing to children when they are young. If typists do not need to think about where keys are, they can devote more energy and attention to their thoughts. And I suspect that familiarity with the concepts of program use will free students from some of the drudgery of learning. People can learn to use computers as adults, but it is likely that early computer users have an easier and freer time on the machines than those who learned as adults, just as people who learn to drive in middle age are often less comfortable and skillful than those who got their license at eighteen.

However, because of the unequal distribution of wealth in most Western countries, all students will not have access to computers (even at greatly reduced prices) if they must own their own machines. And the resources of school districts tend to reflect the economic status of the students in those schools. Furthermore, grants to buy hardware are not enough. Effective instruction in computer literacy depends, I believe, on integrating hardware and software into the classroom under the guidance and expertise of a trained teacher.

Those involved in computer use in writing must take an active role – as teachers, as members of professional organizations, and as politically aware citizens – to expand their own learning and to train others. Teachers are starting to write grants for in-house seminars. Many states have existing groups, such as MECC in Minnesota or the Michigan Association of Computer Users in Learning (MACUL). Professional associations (such as NCTE or CCCC) provide sessions at pre- or post-convention workshops as well as in the regular program. Groups such as NCTE's Assembly for Computers in Education (ACE) or CCCC's Committee on Computers provide leadership by sponsoring publications and displays of software at conventions. Universities host conferences and workshops (often announced in professional journals).

Because of demographic trends, a whole new generation of teachers will soon be entering the schools and universities. Especially important is the teaching of computer use in writing, whether as part of regular classes or in English education classes.

But, inescapably, the major responsibility for equal access to an educational resource lies with the society providing education. "Society," of course, includes parents, individual teachers and schools, universities, companies, foundations, agencies, and legislatures at the local, state, and federal levels of government. The question is not only political; it is ethical as well. Richard Ohmann speculates that "the computer revolution, like other revolutions from the top down, will indeed expand the minds and the freedom of an elite, meanwhile facilitating the degradation of labor and the stratification of the workforce that have been hallmarks of monopoly capitalism from its onset" (683).

The inequities of school district funding must be ameliorated by programs to provide computers as an educational resource and to train teachers in their use. Although leadership should come from local colleges and school districts, support from industry and government must help foster the use of computers in education, and of computers in writing in particular. Research institutions such as Carnegie Mellon and the University of Michigan may work under grants from government and the computer industry to design the hardware of the future, but planning and research must be undertaken to ensure that the existing installed base of computers in the schools can be networked with improved facilities. Teachers and their professional organizations should make their presence known – as an economic force and a reviewing resource for quality control – through users' groups and consortia.

As a teacher involved in the application of computers to writing classes, you have a role to play and an ethical responsibility to act.

The potential of computer technology in education is enormous, but not value-free. In the design of software, the distribution of software, and access to computers, we face ethical dilemmas as we do in any important and far-reaching aspect of our society. In fact, the use of computers in education can and should be seen as part of a larger societal issue. As Carolyn Marvin argues:

> New technologies create conditions for new power struggles, they are the manifest imperfection as well as the marvel of our morality and imagination, they use scarce resources which are then unavailable for other purposes. And this will always be so. . . . New information technologies will be used by the powerful to increase their power unless somebody makes other plans. And just as freedom, security and pleasure have never been easily won in the history of the world, just as that battle is never fully won and must be continually refought, so it is not going to be easy now. But it is going to be important. (24)

The resolution of these problems "does not compute." The challenge and responsibility of ethical choice is and remains uniquely human.

A Theory of One's Own?
An Introduction to Theoretical
and Critical Contexts for
Composition and Computers

Deborah H. Holdstein

———◆———

Recalling in *A Room of One's Own* how she had been barred from the university library, Virginia Woolf notes that while the elitism of male scholarship and methodology made it seem, in Elaine Showalter's words, "unpleasant to be locked out, . . . it was worse, perhaps, to be locked in" ("Feminist Criticism" 244). Woolf's observations have left us a twofold legacy: they make us aware of a hierarchy that persists in academia and yet, in their rejection of that elitism, direct us toward the successful departure point taken by Woolf's feminist descendants.

As did Woolf, we in computers and composition today find ourselves struggling against an academic hierarchy, a ladder of values on which theory and criticism occupy the top rungs; the mid-level rungs belong to "literature" and the like; composition and technical communications sit near the bottom; and on the lowest, battered rungs rests computers and composition. (Teacher training and The Teaching of . . . must share the bottom rung, if they make it to the ladder at all.) It must be emphasized that the order of fields in this essay's title accurately reflects a seemingly inevitable structure that frames the social context in which we conduct our research, strive for tenure and promotion, and teach our students.

Particularly since there is little or no active theory unique to the field, my purpose is briefly to outline several useful, influential theoretical perspectives that may be applied to computers and composition even as they point toward the necessity of a theory primarily developed from within. In this process, the muse of feminist criticism not only instructs by demonstrating a parallel situation but offers a sign of hope. Lillian S. Robinson writes, "The feminist challenge, although intrinsically (and to my mind, refreshingly) polemical, has not been simply a reiterated attack, but a series of suggested alternatives to the male-dominated membership and attitudes of the suggested canon" (573). We can follow how feminist criticism has progressed, in Elaine Showalter's words, from the early, first phases of the personal essay flaunting "its politics and its feelings," to being "independent and intellectually coherent" (*New Feminist* 4).

This does not mean that the struggle is now an easy one, as Annette Kolodny explains: "[I]nstead of being welcomed onto the train, we have been forced to negotiate a minefield. The very energy and diversity of our enterprise have rendered us vulnerable to attack on the grounds that we lack definition and coherence" (502). Similarly, for those of us in the field of computers and composition, personal testimonials concerning the miracles of word processing and perfunctory, sloppy statistical studies of one word-processing experimental group versus the control group can no longer hold. We must attempt to develop a theory base of our own, though we too may begin first, ironically, with the critical contexts of other disciplines. We can then work toward developing our own polemic and define ourselves so that others will not do it for us.

An Interdisciplinary Model

Recent work in technical communications, the first cousin to our field, might serve as a model for solid scholarship and theory in computers and composition. In their introduction to the groundbreaking *New Essays in Technical and Scientific Communication*, Paul V. Anderson, R. John Brockmann, and Carolyn R. Miller recognize "weakness[es] of research in scientific and technical communication, one traceable to the inheritance of previous theory, the other an accident of the way colleges and universities have organized themselves in the twentieth century" (7). The editors call for a stronger research program, more scholarly work based on established research in other fields – linguistics, anthropology, sociology, and philosophy, for example – and not merely articles relating practical experience or, for that matter, work based in literature or philology (9). By challenging the traditional distinction between rhetoric and science, scholars of technical communications can build rich, credible theory; such scholarship, then, could "support and correct teaching strategies and curriculum design" (10; see also Richard VanDeWeghe). Finally, it is their belief that informed theory based on a theoretical subdiscipline can ultimately support and guide the practices of the professional communicator (10). This is the appropriate charge for researcher-teachers in computers and composition: that ideal balance between theory and practice, a solid scholarship that still fosters an undiminished commitment to pedagogy.

We can easily borrow Anderson, Brockmann, and Miller's view that we can enrich our field from disciplines other than literature or literary criticism. This stance challenges C. P. Snow–like assumptions about the divisions between and relative significance of scientific and nonscientific discourse. In *New Essays*, for example, Jack Selzer consults research in reading comprehension and psycho-linguistics, surveying a range of controlled experiments, to attack the traditional emphasis in technical communications courses on the readability research that advises short sentences and short words. In the same volume, Thomas Huckin goes a step further to emphasize process-based research in psychology that exa-mines the ways in which people read and understand. Huckin describes concepts in cognitive research that bear directly on the ways we understand scientific prose (11, introd.). Basing his recommendations on this research, Huckin suggests strate-gies for writers that offer more appropriate guidelines for writers than do tradi-tional notions of readability. We can emulate such research when we in classroom practice acknowledge the dangers of the uninformed use of style analyzers or even spelling checkers; when a writing center tutor puts a student in front of a drill-and-practice program to help her improve her writing; when our students gather around a terminal (or in front of a projection screen) and help one another brain-storm ideas on a topic or rewrite and finally edit a later draft (see the essays by Dobrin and Barker in this volume).

Theories that are process-based or that emphasize the social or interdisciplin-ary nature of discourse offer appropriate foundations for our work. In yet an-other theory-based paper that challenges traditional classroom practice (practice based on misperceptions of the "functional, practical, formattable" limitations of technical communications), Victoria Winkler (now Victoria Mikelonis) balances the process approach of recent composition theory with the more product-oriented approach that relies on formal models; Winkler argues that process can inform product, and that the two elements are not mutually exclusive. We might explore how those less-than-stellar icons of "product" – drill-and-practice software – become part of process-oriented instruction and assist students who find it useful; we can examine, too, how the instructor, peer tutor, or student writer might make the leap between product and process.

Using philosophical theory, David N. Dobrin's "What's Technical about Tech-nical Writing?" offers an alternative definition of technical communications by placing the field within a new social and academic context. This critical strategy naturally suggests the potential for peer revision groups working at the computer. By extension, we might examine the social and political implications of collabora-tive writing in a computer laboratory; of privacy and the ethics of access (and nonaccess); of the advantages of previous exposure among privileged students in a writing classroom where computer use is required; and of a classroom in which all students draft, compose, revise, and edit their essays at the terminal (see Schwartz, in this volume).

Perhaps the most significant piece among the interdisciplinary work in techni-cal communications is Charles Bazerman's "Scientific Writing as a Social Act." Drawing on the work of Karl Popper, Imre Lakatos, Stephen Toulmin, Thomas Kuhn, and Ludwig Fleck, among others, Bazerman concludes that "however we conceive scientific writing, scientific texts, and the processes of dissemination and reception, our conception must always be grounded in an understanding of the contemporary social and intellectual conditions that surround any act of statement-making" (176). Similarly, Lee Odell warns in his essay "Beyond the Text":

> We have scarcely begun to understand how organizational context relates to writing and we have almost no information about which aspects of that relationship are helpful to writers and which are harmful. Thus, we must test each new finding in this area, trying to reconcile it with our best intuitions as classroom teachers and with our best theory about how and why people write and about what it means to be a mature, effective writer. (278)

Both Bazerman and Odell work toward new conceptions of technical communications as a discipline and demand that teacher-researchers reexamine the ways in which they structure courses, teach students, and transfer research and scholarship to classroom practice. As Bazerman invokes recent sociological theory to inform technical communications, so, too, can it support a theoretical base for computers and composition. Fortunately, that interdisciplinary relationship has begun (see, for instance, Herrmann, "Ethnographic Study"; Faigley, "Nonacademic"; Selfe, in this volume).

The Social Context of Learning

There is an additional argument for multidisciplinary contexts to enhance theory and research. As literary criticism and other disciplines, such as sociology, have taught us in recent years (see Fish; Bazerman, "Scientific"; Faigley, "Nonacademic"; Miller; and Dobrin, "What's Technical" and "Is Technical" among others), we all work within contexts that are learned, social, and political at the same time: hence it is important to acknowledge these contexts when we formulate theories about, or conduct research in, computers and composition (or, for that matter, when we formulate a process-based curriculum for our students). Social contexts inevitably lead to political ones: that the New Critics spouted forth from the University of Chicago and not from the lesser lights of the neighboring colleges on the South Side of Chicago can be seen as more than just an accidental factor in the prominence and wide acceptance their theories attained. (For a discussion of these political and social issues as they relate to composition and computers, see Selfe, in this volume; Holdstein, *On Composition*.)

Certainly the recent turn from positivism-formalism toward pluralism, reader-response criticism, and Marxist criticism, for example, can provide standards for our theory and practice, by affirming our classroom emphasis on multiple drafts and multiple responses to drafts; on peer revision groups; on a concern with gender, race, and class in our writing and teaching; and on other process-based, theory-influenced goals with which we teach composition. At the same time, in a political sense, these standards can take us beyond our equivalent of the readability formulas of technical communications (just as researchers in that field have moved ahead), beyond the notion that work in computers and composition is merely "practical, functional" discourse, to raise our level of credibility as a discipline within the academy.

Recent reader-response criticism articulates a useful social view of knowledge that can enrich scholarly work in computers and composition. Unlike New Critics and other theorists who affirm the sanctity and isolation of the text from other influence or context, critics such as Stanley Fish, Wolfgang Iser (*Act*), and Louise Rosenblatt look to psychology and sociology for more appropriate views of writing and knowing as context- and experience-based. Iser, for instance, finds that reading is an interaction between our gestalten (views, perspectives) of the text that influence the ways in which we make sense of that text, and our gestalten that are changed or rethought because of the text. If we expand Iser's discussion, we can consider how our gestalten are transformed when we compose and revise texts exclusively at the computer and whether the way we work differs when we compose at the terminal, revise in ink on hard copy, and enter our changes (revising, as well, as we go along).

Rosenblatt holds a "transactional" view, asserting that the act of perceiving the verbal and visual cues of a text triggers "the poem" readers "make"; the interpretation of the work depends on psychological, social, and other contexts of experience that the readers bring along as they read. And in *Is There a Text in This Class?* (is there a word processor in this class?), Stanley Fish acknowledges the subjectivity of the reader's response to a text. Fish distinguishes between the "subjective and idiosyncratic" aspects of reading and "the level of response everyone shares," or interpretation; knowledge, then, is based on a type of response that will be common to a community, a community that considers a "certain response a valid interpretation – or knowledge" (5). He attacks that aspect of traditional literary study in which "students are trained to . . . recognize and then 'discount' whatever was unique and personal in their response so that there would be nothing between them and the exertion of the text's control" (7).

Fish, too, understands all knowledge as socially dependent: "[A]ll facts are discourse specific . . . no one can claim for any language a special relationship to the facts as they 'simply are,' unmediated by social or conventional assumptions" (199). In teaching, then, knowledge isn't formulaic or divinely written; rather, it must be devised through the interaction of the class as a community of interpreters and institutions. If so, community interactions must change when peer revision groups become electronically centered. Researchers in composition and computers should examine the nature of the change and consider how the influence on students differs from that within a computer-supported composition class when they return to their discipline-specific communities, particularly after writing-across-the-disciplines courses.

Building on work in the philosophy of language, David Bleich suggests that interpretation resymbolizes experience at both personal and community levels. The social community of the classroom allows for social adaptation and growth. In "Discerning Motives in Language Use," he argues that subjective and social bases for resymbolization should form the foundation of all writing instruction, as well as of literary research. How is the balance between personal and community changed – or how are these two levels affected and influenced – by the computer-supported writing community as distinct from the traditional writing classroom?

A Place at the Table?

Metatheory and the study of institutional history have a useful, albeit often a vicarious and ironic, place in discussing professional implications for work in computers and composition. In his review of Gerald Graff's *Professing Literature*, Paul Jay defines the field:

> Critical theory, while it may be thought of by many as wholly concerned with theories and methods of textual analysis, raises questions that lead inevitably to an examination of the very institutions and professions that engage in such analysis. . . . It is simply not possible to read critical texts in a Derridean fashion, for example, without eventually analyzing the *institutional* history of its language, without tracing the ways in which critical *concepts* both discipline, and are disciplined by, the institution of English studies. (119)

While composition theorists might well use Graff's assertion that theory must be part of every classroom, with students being let "in on whatever matters of principle are at issue to them" (251–52), to reinforce the contention that theory is central to what we do (and I've extended the latter phrase, a variation on Jay's words, since he refers only to those who "do" literature), we might also find blatant irony in Graff's regret that theory is "ghettoized" in literature departments. In Graff's view, "we can expect literary theory to be defused not by being repressed but by being accepted and quietly assimilated . . . where it ceases to be a bother" (249); once "part of a department's table of areas," literary theory might develop into "a private enclave in which theorists speak only to one another" unless it becomes a central part of literary study (251). This analysis by implication limits the "table of areas" to literature, criticism, and theory. Composition theorists, informing our work, generating our theory with literary and literary-critical contexts, should examine, as feminist literary critics have before them, whether they wish to seek a chair at the table or to continue to speak (mostly) only to each other (see Kolodny; L. S. Robinson; Hull, Scott, and Smith, for example).

We can hope that those of us investigating the effectiveness of word processing are looking at the work not only of those involved almost exclusively with computers and composition but of those writing about the composing process itself. The most interesting work – "useful" in terms of generating richer theory and more appropriate classroom practices – includes the thinking of Peter Elbow, Janet Emig (*Composing Processes*), Donald M. Murray ("Teaching the Other Self"), James

Moffett, and Sondra Perl, among others. Elbow, for instance, has students continually write and read aloud for direct and immediate feedback from the class—the audience, a group with shared knowledge, assumptions, and concerns. Similarly, Anne Herrington sees the "classroom as social forum"; Murray teaches writing as a social process by having his students try to "internalize" the criticism of their audience during peer review. And since 1970—with Richard E. Young, A. L. Becker, and Kenneth L. Pike's *Rhetoric*; Emig's landmark study on the composing processes of twelfth graders; and Janet Lauer's bibliography on heuristics and composition—composition specialists have begun to acknowledge the process of writing and its social contexts and influences instead of emphasizing only its product.

As this is but a small sample of important work that could influence not only our practice but the thinking that should support our practice, we must wonder about the substantive, scholarship-based preparation of those in learning centers, say, who would use drill and practice to replace one-on-one tutoring (that is, without incorporating the lesson into the actual process of writing). Perhaps part of the fault lies in the scarcity of theory-based scholarship until recently; perhaps it is simpler to overemphasize the field's two flagship journals, *College Composition and Communication* and *College English*, rather than extend our view toward newer, less-familiar journals (such as *Computers and Composition*, *Rhetoric Review*, *Journal of Advanced Composition*, *Writing Teacher*, and *Writing Program Administration*) with important contributions in several areas that include computers and composition. It is also the natural if unfortunate inclination of some to look almost exclusively to the textbook for teaching practice with and without the computer: fortunately, excellent texts, such as Helen J. Schwartz's *Interactive Writing* and Ronald Sudol's *Textfiles* are process- and reader-based, providing the appropriate emphasis for using the computer to enhance writing as a process.

What We Have to Offer

But even as we assert our differences as a specialization within writing, acknowledge our ties through interdisciplinary and social-based theory or research, and raise interesting issues for theory and research in our own field that stem from these contexts, we must be able to offer something else of substance to other fields. What might that be?

While much of our theory might seem derivative (and that's not a bad thing), indigenous to computers and composition—as perhaps to technical communications—is the use of visual information to convey meaning. In 1984, S. M. Halloran and A. N. Bradford noted that "while technical and scientific writing is primarily visual, no writing can ever divorce itself entirely from the auditory mode . . . " (191). Here, the authors emphasize the auditory over the visual; yet within the social context of much composition theory, speech can unite the visual and the written. If we observe that reading the text on a computer screen aloud affects the composing process, and affects it differently from reading the text on one's own or with a group or from pen and paper, our field should examine the theoretical implications of such classroom investigations. An example would be the use of supertext: how will text and our perceptions of text alter when we see it on a screen; when we window over it to add reminder notes; when we pull down menus or use computer-screen notecards; when we write different types of discourse? And what of that new wrinkle on our computer screens, one that changes the ways in which text is perceived and manipulated – hypertext?

Yet another frontier for our scholarship might involve give-and-take with our earlier muse, feminist criticism, including approaches to writing, to the reader, to the text; to issues of *écriture féminine*, "a way of talking about women's writing that preserves the value of the feminine," while asserting its difference (Showalter, "Feminist Criticism" 249); to the question of whether – and, if so, how – gender shapes the computer-generated text as opposed to the handwritten; to gender differences within electronically supported peer revision groups; to gender and hypertext. How might differences in the gender of professionals writing computer documentation and engineering and technical communications draw attention in those communities to what Showalter calls "the philosophical, linguistic, and practical problems of women's use of language?" (253). Showalter also notes that "the debate over language is one of the most exciting areas in gynocritics" (253), the specialized critical discourse that studies women as writers. What about computer gynocritics? Just as feminist criticism, in the words of Kolodny, has resulted in "an acute attentiveness to the ways in which certain power relations, usually those in which males wield various forms of influence over females, are inscribed in texts (both literary and critical) . . . as the unquestioned, often unacknowledged given of the culture" (501), we should begin to study how these power relations operate in our research, writing, and classrooms.

Feminist and Marxist critics (see, e.g., Showalter, "Feminist Criticism"; Gilbert; Eagleton), among others, have argued that we must enlarge the canon of what we consider to be great literature. Lillian S. Robinson's warning to feminist critics aptly serves those in computers and composition as well: "[I]n one sense, the more coherent our sense of female tradition is, the stronger will be our eventual case. Yet the longer we wait, the more comfortable the women's literature ghetto – separate, apparently autonomous, and far from equal – may begin to feel" (581). As Cary Nelson noted in his 1987 MLA address, the canon empowers and disempowers, establishing the terms of power. We must evaluate our own scholarly canon. We can reassert the value of rhetoric over poetics, the dominant concern of the last century; our traditional rhetoric must embrace visual rhetoric, an emphasis important to theory as well as practice. Thus as literary criticism, feminist literary criticism, the larger fields of composition theory and technical communications, philosophy, and sociology help us enlarge our theoretical and pedagogical canon, our colleagues in those fields might enhance theirs by observing a field creating its own valuable scholarship, demonstrating substantive research and theory and, by implication, a more informed pedagogy.

But first we must redefine ourselves, rather than continue within the academy as others define us. In *Criticism in the Wilderness*, Geoffrey Hartman deconstructs, so to speak, the traditional distinction between literature and criticism, and we might apply this perspective to composition versus literature, technical communications versus literature – the dichotomies we live by – and composition versus computers (with other combinations thereof). Eagleton goes several steps further in *Literary Theory*, suggesting an ideal curriculum that studies various types of discourse, all the while illustrating their social effects. While Eagleton, Wayne Booth, and others call for enlargement of the curriculum, we will not see such an invitation extended to research in computers and composition by those empowered by the academic hierarchy until we write from solid theoretical contexts. Adapting David Bartholomae's altar call for empowering our students, we within the academy must accept the dictates of that structure before we can find our own voices and, perhaps, later reject that structure and its conventions; like our students, we must become aware that our "initial progress" as scholars will "be marked by . . . abilities to take on the role of privilege, by . . . abilities to establish authority" (162).

As Winkler writes, "A good theory is eminently practical" (111). Scholarship in computers and composition has already begun to progress, to inform writing-as-process to reach scholarly mainstreams and influence our classroom practice beyond those tips for creating files and formatting memos and those glowing testimonials to CAI or word processing. Showalter notes, "[I]f the women's movement has taught us anything, it is that we must all share the housework but must also get the chance to gaze at the stars" (*New Feminist* 16). At the same time, we will not lose touch with our students as we emphasize theory. Rather, the potential for computers and composition to rise as a respected, if initially modest, field within the academy might enable us to redefine and "reconnote" the ways in which our discipline can provide contexts for scholarship as well as borrow them. For only then, with theory-based scholarship and practice, will we be truly "useful" to our students as teacher-scholars within the not-so-often friendly confines of the academy.

A Limitation on the Use
of Computers in Composition

David N. Dobrin

———◆———

In this article, I make a distinction between two kinds of computer programs: those meant to respond to the form of a text and those meant to respond to the meaning. I will argue that the latter are not and will not be useful in composition. This limitation exists because computers can respond only to the form of a text, not to its meaning, and thus any apparent response to the meaning is a simulation or approximation. This simulation is inevitably inaccurate. This inaccuracy makes most such programs useless.[1]

You can get an intuitive grasp of this distinction by looking at table 1. The applications in the first group merely manipulate symbols. For each, what the symbols mean (usually) doesn't affect their operation. A communications application like electronic mail, for instance, sends any string of characters, be it random groups of letters or a Chinese transliteration, just as easily as it sends English text. A word processor, too, displays any string equally well. And a spelling checker checks any string for spelling errors equally thoroughly; correctly designed, it can be equally useful on any string.

Both of the latter two applications, however, can occasionally be asked to respond to meaning, and when they are, they don't behave accurately, at least as far as the user is concerned. Word processors, for instance, usually have a command like "Delete this sentence." This command can only work on text, because it can only work when there are sentences. What counts as a sentence depends on the meaning; hence successful execution of the command requires a response to meaning. The word processor, however, only simulates the response. (Usually it looks for a period followed by two spaces.) When the simulation fails (when, say, it finds a mistyped *Mr.*), it deletes two sentences or half a sentence rather than one. Similarly, when spelling checkers are asked to check spelling, they only check form, not meaning, and the simulation fails (on homonyms, for instance) when a judgment about meaning is required.

The applications in the second group in the table (style analyzers, idea processors, and invention aids) can only work on a meaningful text. (Random groups

Table 1

Applications That Usually Respond to Form

Application	Accuracy	Flexibility	Utility
Electronic Mail	100%	No response to meaning	Great
Word Processing	98%	Meaning defines some formal characteristics of text	Great
Spelling Checkers	94%	Correctness of spelling determined by meaning	Good

Applications That Imitate a Response to Meaning

Application	Accuracy	Flexibility	Utility
Style Analyzers	Poor	Parsing is poor, and analysis of results requires reference to meaning	Little
Idea Processors	–	Inflexible because not adaptable to the meaning of the context	Little
Invention Aids	Poor	Inflexible because probing of ideas requires an understanding of the writer's meaning	Little

of letters might have a correct spelling, but they have no style, are never misused, and never express a mistaken or banal idea.) These applications, I am arguing, are not even reasonably accurate. Without accuracy, they are useless.

My argument is divided into two parts. In the first, I describe the utility (or lack thereof) of some current programs in both the first group and the second group; in the second, the possibilities for improvement. Let me admit in advance that each of my arguments, the one about utility and the one about the future, has a built-in structural problem. Problem 1: when someone says a tool is useless, that does not mean that the tool can never be used in a certain way. Arguments about utility are about whether a tool can be used in a reasonable way and at a reasonable cost for its intended purpose. One might use a sledgehammer to hit a baseball, but as a baseball-hitting tool, sledgehammers are useless – that is, too expensive and too inefficient (heavy!) to be useful. When we read *Consumer Reports*, we take this idea about utility for granted. But when the intended use isn't clear-cut or when the tools themselves are unfamiliar, people can easily get into wrangles of the form, "Well, I use it, so it must be useful." Such a response is not a reply to my argument.

Problem 2 will be described further on.

Syntactic Labels for Meaningful Objects

What do I mean when I say that a computer responds only to the form of a text? Take as a sample text the letter *A*, which I just typed into the computer. My *A* is a meaningful object, part of the English alphabet, with a certain sound attached to it. The computer does not actually handle the letter *A* qua letter *A*. Instead, it attaches a syntactic label to the letter and manipulates the label. This syntactic label (let's call it 'letter A') has no position in the alphabet and no sound associated with it.[2] To attach such a label is to "define" the meaningful object "syntactically"– that is, according to its "form" or "shape," or according to "syntactic rules."[3]

Computers handle any meaningful object by defining it syntactically, often by combining labels. A 'word', for instance, is defined as a collection of 'letters' surrounded by 'spaces' or 'punctuation marks'. A sentence is a string of 'words' concluded by a 'period', 'question mark', or 'colon' and two 'spaces'. A 'correctly spelled word' is any 'word' which also appears on a master list of 'correctly spelled words' in the computer's dictionary.

These syntactic definitions do not always correspond to our definitions; the response to form is not the same as the response to meaning. The computer (mine, anyway) labels *bbbcsgeds*, *SDI*, and *PresidentReagan* as single 'words', and it treats *clear-cut* as two words. The computer does not treat this sentence as a single sentence: for the computer, it is two. And the computer does not call *diatome* or *natatorium* 'correctly spelled.' This lack of correspondence between what the computer does and what we do is in the nature of things. Meaningful objects are defined by their meaning, not by satisfying syntactic rules.

But this lack of correspondence has several consequences. First, while any particular object may in fact be correctly labeled, it is not possible to build a system that can label every object correctly. Second, in any application in which the labeling is unreliable, the user has to compensate for the errors of the computer. Third, if the errors are not clear-cut and relatively infrequent, the utility of having the program make those labels is lost.

Rather than prove this point, I want to demonstrate it. In the next two sections of this essay, I will describe several different programs, show how errors enter in, and describe the ways of compensating for the errors.

By rights I ought to demonstrate the point for each type of program mentioned in table 1. To do so, however, would be tedious. The inaccuracies and consequent difficulties of style checkers emerge in a different way from the inaccuracies and difficulties of idea processors or invention aids, and they don't emerge at all until you're well down in the nitty-gritty. For each kind of program, you need a loupe to see the problems with any clarity (see Dobrin, *Writing*, "Don't Throw Out Your Dictionary Yet," "Searching for Mr. Goodcheck").

Compensating for Errors in Word Processors and Spelling Checkers

Word processors make mistakes about sentences because their formal definition of a sentence is very weak. It is based entirely on a statistical correlation between occurrences of word groups that match the computer's formal definition of a sentence and the occurrence of sentences in the text, not on anything intrinsic. The correlation is, admittedly, quite high. Eighty percent of the 'sentences' flagged by the computer in this article thus far are in fact sentences; the command works correctly eighty percent of the time. Still, the twenty percent of the time it doesn't, the user experiences some difficulties. Right now, the user just has to cope.

Could the technology be improved? Certainly, some accuracy could be gained by improving the formal definition. You could, for instance, take each 'word' in a putative 'sentence' and determine its 'part of speech', using the computer's dictionary. With this information, you could begin parsing by, say, testing each potential sentence group for the presence of at least one free noun and verb. Neither the determination of parts of speech nor the initial parsing would be entirely accurate, but if you added still more rules – for instance, that only adjectives and nouns can follow prepositions – you could refine the process. Eventually, by adding thousands of rules, you could get a system that, though still not perfect,[4] would have considerably higher accuracy.

A word-processing system that incorporated this feature, however, would not be a useful tool. Making such calculations costs enormous amounts of computer time and memory. It's much faster and easier to have the human compensate.

With spelling checkers, too, it's much easier to have the human correct the errors. But with these applications, the difficulty of compensating for the computer's errors is greater. Spelling checkers work by seeing whether a 'word' in the text exactly matches a 'word' in the computer's dictionary. When we use the spelling checker, we are relying on yet another statistical correlation, one between mismatches and incorrectly spelled words. This correlation is high, but not perfect. The following is a list of 'incorrectly spelled words' I got by running my spelling checker (the standard UNIX) on the text thus far:

> analyze
> Analyzers
> adjectives
> bbbcsgeds
> diatome
> Fodor
> judgment
> natatorium
> putative
> SDI
> Solipsism

The errors the computer makes fall into several categories. In one are correctly spelled words absent from the computer's dictionary (like *natatorium*). In another are proper names (*Fodor*), abbreviations (*SDI*), and made-up words (*bbbcsgeds*). Another consists of nonstandard but acceptable spellings (*gage* for *gauge*), nonconventional forms of spelling (*s-p-e-l-l*), and foreign words, none of which happen to be on the list. In the last category are the words that are absent from the list above but shouldn't be: *PresidentReagan*, for some odd reason was not caught.

Also absent would be any incorrectly spelled 'words' witch (for instance) match some other 'word' in the dictionary or which match an incorrectly spelled word which has accidentally been inserted in the dictionary.

Admittedly, these errors are not serious. There were some seventeen hundred words and only ten-odd errors on the list, plus of course those that weren't caught, if any. The accuracy, therefore, is much better than that of word processors. Alas, the difficulty of making up for the inaccuracies is also greater.

In the list, the computer errors (the garbage and the phantom errors) greatly outnumber the actual errors; what I call the "garbage ratio" is high. To use the list above, I have to pick through the garbage. In theory, what counts as garbage and what doesn't is completely decidable; I can always tell whether a word is misspelled by looking in a real dictionary. But I usually don't look in the dictionary – too time-consuming. Instead, I pass words if they seem to fall into one of the categories I listed. If, for instance, a word looks correctly spelled and it's so uncommon that the computer dictionary probably wouldn't have it, I assume it is correctly spelled. Did you do this too? Or did you see that *diatome* was in fact misspelled? (It should be *diatom*.)

Whether you did or didn't, look at the structure of our response to the program. Because the computer makes errors, we must pick through the garbage before we can use the output. If we know what we are doing, we can sift fairly rapidly. But where we are in some doubt – or even just overconfident – we will make mistakes. Indeed, because we trust ourselves more than the program, only our inadvertent errors will leap out at us; in effect, a spelling checker is most useful as a typo checker. For me, though, typo checkers aren't all that useful. All three of my spelling checkers take time to use, I have to proofread anyway, and typos leap out from the text, too. Only when I particularly need a typo checker – for instance, just before I send something out – do I use the spelling checker.

You and I are probably pretty good spellers, and so our garbage ratio is high, because most catches will be computer errors, not ours. What about when the garbage ratio is lower? Does the program become more useful as a spelling checker? This is an interesting question, which probably requires some empirical research to answer. But I can suggest the shape of the answer. From the point of view of the user, there are three kinds of words on the list: the catches (inadvertent errors), the obvious garbage (*adjective*), and the problem words (*diatome*), which the user is not sure what to do about. The user can react to these problem words in two ways: One, he or she can fail to recognize that there is in fact a problem. Two, the user can see the problem and try to resolve the uncertainty. If the problem goes unrecognized, the user is no worse off than before, except that running the program takes time and encourages the idea that the spelling in the text is accurate. If the problem is recognized, the user again has options. He or she can look the word up in the dictionary. If that happens, it is a good result. Or, the user can just change the word to something he or she knows how to spell. This is a pernicious result. Assuming that the user learns this response and respects it, the word is effectively removed from his or her written vocabulary.

If the problem words were always those that were misspelled, the benefits might still be substantial; after all, writers would only be losing words they were unsure of anyway. But many problem words are correctly spelled (*natatorium*); they appear only because the computer doesn't recognize them. In weighing the costs and benefits, we have to include the cost of having doubt cast on correct spellings and the consequent attrition of those words. Thus the utility of spelling programs for bad spellers depends on whether they doggedly look up the words; that's why the question is empirical. If they do, they will learn; if they don't, they could well be hurt. In my (limited) experience, people do not look up words. In two years of working with students in the MIT computer rooms, I never saw a dictionary besides mine in the room. I have often seen students use spelling checkers, and I have often seen them change words rather than look up the correct spelling.

I have noticed one other problem with spelling checkers, a problem for me and a problem for the students. In a peculiar way, they are a distraction. Waiting for the occasionally slow checker to finish, poking through the garbage, and figuring out which errors the computer made are not very fruitful activities. Worse, when I'm feeling particularly lazy, I use the spelling checker as an excuse for not proofreading. I figure that I've reduced the number of errors and thus there is less reason to go back. As far as I can tell, the students feel that way, too.

Still, I am in the minority. For most people, the benefits outweigh the costs. Notice, though, that the balance shifts if the frequency of problem words increases or if dealing with problem words gets even harder. This is exactly what happens with other kinds of error checkers, like usage checkers. They, too, generate lists of mismatching words or phrases, but the mismatches are rarely inadvertent, and the number of phantom errors is considerably larger. With usage checkers, moreover, there is no simple way of deciding the status of problem words. Do the benefits still outweigh the costs?

Text Analysis Programs

Let me now turn to usage checkers, programs that check your diction, style, or grammar. These, unlike spelling checkers, are text analysis programs, because they are designed to respond to meaning. For these programs, the structure of the user's response is the same as that to spelling checkers. Unfortunately, though, the benefits are markedly diminished and the costs markedly increased. People generally don't make many inadvertent errors in usage (as distinct from errors of ignorance); neither do usage manuals have the authority or clarity of the dictionary. Thus what counts as an error is much less clear-cut. At the same time, the garbage ratio goes way up. For all these reasons, such programs encourage misuse, and the kinds of misuse encouraged are far more probable and more pernicious. Let me take as examples two text analysis programs widely considered to be the state of the art: *Diction* and *Style*, two of the *Writer's Workbench* programs put out by Bell Labs (Cherry).

Diction works exactly the way spelling checkers do. Instead of a list of 'correctly spelled words', it has a list of 'words and phrases frequently misused'. When it runs through a text, it finds and flags occurrences of those phrases. I'll show you some phrases it caught in this text. Let me caution you that I write in a somewhat breezy, slangy way, and that the *Writer's Workbench* is not particularly sympathetic to that kind of style.

Partial Output of the *Diction* Program Run on this Paper Thus Far
Computers handle any *[meaningful]* object by defining it syntactically, often by combining labels.
This is an interesting question, *[which]* probably requires some empirical research to answer.
The computer does not *[actually]* handle the letter *A* qua letter *A*.
Did you see that *diatome* was *[in fact]* misspelled?
The *Writer's Workbench* is not particularly sympathetic to that *[kind of]* style.
number of sentences 133 number of phrases found 36

Some other words or phrases flagged by the *Writer's Workbench* are *all of, anticipate, the author, but that, construct, decide on, decide upon, in order to, number of, sophisticated, upon,* and *very.*

Like the spelling checker, this program depends on a statistical correlation between the occurrence of the 'phrases' and an error in diction. Users have to respond to the program, therefore, the way they do to spelling checkers—with suspicion. The inadvertent errors are caught; the problem entries create problems. The garbage ratio for this program, however, varies even more dramatically from writer to writer than it does for spelling checkers. For a good writer, the extensive output—typically a third of my sentences are flagged—is pure garbage. For a bad writer, the output is still mostly garbage, because the words on the list are much more likely to be used correctly than to be misused. But there will be some catches.

Unhappily for the bad writer, these catches will almost always pose problems. People most often misuse words out of ignorance, as we said, and not inadvertence. With the problem catch, the user knows something may be wrong but does not know what the error is and does not know how to fix it. The greater the ignorance, the greater the number of problem words, and the more difficult they are to cope with. Remember that to reduce the number of problem words to manageable size, one must know how the program works, just as one must with spelling checkers. When I first used *Diction*, I fretted, for instance, about whether to use *decide upon*, or *decide on*. A student of mine didn't know that *sophisticated* is sometimes considered an overused intensive; when it was flagged, he changed the word, because he thought he had made a subtle mistake in usage, like using *anticipate* when one means *expect.* Even to use the program, then, one needs some instruction in how to use problem words correctly. But if one has that instruction, one doesn't need the program.

The user of the spelling checker can, in extremis, turn to the dictionary. Is there a similarly reliable resource here? Yes and no. Grammar and usage manuals are available, but they are tedious, hard to understand, and very hard to apply. The makers of *Writer's Workbench* apparently recognize this; they supply a companion program, called *Explain*, which does suggest alternates. (*Decide* for *decide on*, *on* for *upon*, *many* for *a number of*, *expect* for *anticipate*, and nothing at all for *sophisticated*.) A writer can test the alternates and, if they seem to work, use them. (But even then the writer must have an understanding of the language. In the sentence "To be a good chess player, one must anticipate the opponent's moves," how many people who don't know the difference between the two verbs, will realize that, this time, they should use *anticipate*, rather than *expect*?)

So if you don't know what you're doing and you see a flag, what's your safest strategy? Obviously, to do just what my student did, change the flagged word, whether it needs it or not. Do most users operate this way? Lorinda Cherry (the author of the program), in the original documentation for *Diction*, says that in its first release, between fifty and sixty percent of the flagged errors were actually made. Fifty to sixty percent. Try an experiment. Show someone unfamiliar with grammar rules the sentences from this essay that *Diction* flagged and ask that person to correct those that need revision. See what happens when the uninitiated are alerted to the possibility of an error.

Perhaps the program is not meant to be used unaided. Perhaps it should only be used as part of a pedagogical program. The students would be taught the correct use of problem words; the program would then remind them that these are pitfall areas. If these errors were important, such a pedagogical program might be useful. But they're not that important. Such a program merely brings *kind of* versus *rather* problems into undue prominence and takes time away from more important concerns. True, the existence of the program makes it tempting for a teacher to spend time on such matters. But that temptation should be resisted. The program is merely a distraction. It doesn't exist because texts cry out for it; it exists only because it is relatively easy to create.

To realize how much of a distraction this program can be, consider the experience I had in writing this article. I had to run *Diction* many, many times, because I had to make sure that the sentences it found stayed through the revisions. I thus had to look very carefully at the sentences it flagged. I found that I often revised those sentences, more often than I revised others. Not once did I make the changes that *Diction* recommended. Instead, I found and corrected other errors. I found them, I think, because the sentences were brought to my attention. Consider the implications of this. A program that flagged sentences randomly might well inspire more and better corrections than the *Diction* program.[5]

If we can't get humans to compensate for the errors in *Diction* or in spelling checkers, can we get the computer to? The answer is in the next section.

One way of thinking about the problem *Diction* poses is to say that too much has been concluded about usage errors on flimsy statistical evidence. Possible usage errors are identified as such when the probability that they are in fact errors may be abysmally low. One way of getting around this problem is to give statistics without making any strong suggestions about what they mean. This approach is taken by the Bell Labs' *Style* program.

Style calculates statistics about style by attaching syntactic labels like 'noun' and 'verb' to each word, in much the way described above. It then counts the number of each kind of 'part of speech', number of free and clausal noun-verb sequences, and so on. Accuracy is not great, but the output, as you'll see, doesn't require accuracy.[6] I'll give you the output of the *Style* program run on an earlier draft of this article up to the beginning of the previous paragraph.

Output of the *Style* Program Run on this Paper Thus Far
readability grades:
(Kincaid) 9.6 (auto) 9.9 (Coleman-Liau) 10.0 (Flesch) 10.1 (59.6)
sentence info:
no. sent 163 no. wds 3081
av sent leng 18.9 av word leng 4.65
no. questions 6 no. imperatives 0
no. nonfunc wds 1705 55.3% av leng 6.12
short sent (<14) 37% (60) long sent (>29) 11% (18)
longest sent 84 wds at sent 1; shortest sent 4 wds at sent 24
sentence types:
simple 38% (62) complex 39% (63)
compound 9% (15) compound-complex 14% (23)
word usage:
verb types as % of total verbs
tobe 41% (169) aux 18% (75) inf 15% (63)
passives as % of non-inf verbs 10% (36)
types as % of total
prep 9.3% (287) conj 2.7% (84) adv 6.5% (200)
noun 25.6% (790) adj 13.5% (416) pron 8.9% (275)
nominalizations 2% (47)
sentence beginnings:
subject opener: noun (52) pron (28) pos (0) adj (11) art (20) tot 68%
prep 6% (10) adv 10% (17)
verb 1% (2) sub_conj 9% (15) conj 2% (3)
expletives 3% (5)

This output looks imposing, but it doesn't mean anything. Here are some questions it doesn't and can't answer. Given my purpose, audience, and style, should I increase or decrease the percentage of nominal sentence openers? Is my passive count too high or too low? What about my *to be* verb count? And if any of these are out of line, what should I do? How much variation in the figures is significant? The Flesch score (is 10.0 good or bad?) varies by as much as a grade level from draft to draft; does that mean that I'm changing my style each time? Indeed, do any of the figures tell me anything significant?

To answer these questions, one would have to have an extraordinarily fine-tuned idea of the relation of statistical information to the quality of texts – adjusted, of course, for purpose, audience, and style. I don't have that, and neither, I suspect, do you. Some versions of the program do offer a listing of normal ranges (compiled from Bell Labs technical documents!), but using that listing to detect errors is like cutting diamonds with a wood saw. Notice, too, that if you did have a keen statistical sense, so that a difference of 1 in the Flesch score was important to you, then the inaccuracy of the Bell Labs list would be a great problem.

The makers of the program argue that the figures do tell a less *[sophisticated]* user something. A writer whose Flesch readability score is 15.0 (the authors of the *Federalist Papers*, say Cherry and Vesterman [9]) or a writer whose average sentence length is 38.4 needs to be told that the figures fall well outside normal bounds. I agree that such writers may need help. But they won't be helped in any fundamental way by being told to put in a bunch of periods. The writers should be shortening not just any sentences, but the right sentences. But for the program to tell them which sentences, it would have to be able to respond to meaning, something it can't do.

The objections to *Style*, then, are the same as those to *Diction*. The user has to be able to interpret the output before using the program; the people who can do so don't need it, and the people who can't, can't use it. Like *Diction, Style* can be taught, and then its usefulness would improve. But if *Style* can be taught, so, too, can style, and time is better spent teaching the latter. *Style*, like *Diction*, is a distraction.[7]

Is there any empirical evidence to support the claim that the *Style* program is a distraction? After this article was finished, "The Writer's Workbench *Style* Module as a Predictor of Holistic Writing Evaluations," a study done by Robert S. Hart and Frank Hodgins at the University of Illinois, Champaign-Urbana, came to my attention. Hart and Hodgins took student essays, ran *Style* on them, and then asked whether the *Style* figures predicted the grades the students would get on the essays. The usual problems with consistency of grading among essays and among teachers taken care of, the authors could determine how much the *Writer's Workbench* scores influenced the final grade. They used a standard statistical measure called the r^2, which means the percentage of a change in one figure that can be accounted for (that correlates with) a change in another figure. A high r^2 (correlation) is in the nineties; that is the correlation between the movement in the price of an aggressive mutual fund and the movement in the price of the market. A rough correlation, one with little predictive value, is in the fifties – the correlation between people's heights and their weights. The two do correlate to some extent, but there are wide variations.

Hart and Hodgins found that, for advanced writers, *Writer's Workbench* scores and grades correlated with an r^2 of eleven percent; that is, there was virtually no correlation. (For those of you who are curious, this finding has no negative correlation, that is, grades also don't move inversely with the *Writer's Workbench* scores.) For basic writers, the r^2 was a much higher thirty-seven percent. This might have shown the glimmerings of a possible slight correlation, except that when the researchers tried to cash out the results and determine which *Writer's Workbench* statistics correlated with the grades, they found only a few that had any predictive power, and those few varied from teacher to teacher.[8]

This should not be surprising. Good grades, I am thankful, are given for making good, sensible arguments, not for writing sentences with an average length of seventeen words.

Improving *Style* and *Diction*: *Epistle*

Style and *Diction* are attempts at simulating human response to the meaning of text. They work by identifying some formal characteristics of what humans call "bad usage" or "ornate style" and then flagging text that has those characteristics. Unfortunately, when the writer is skillful, text that the program marks as faulty is usually fine; the output of the program is mostly garbage. The less skillful writers are, the harder they find it to sort through the garbage or to respond appropriately. Even if they could sort through the garbage effectively, the programs still would be distracting and would, I might add, give a not-so-skillful writer the wrong idea about how problems are identified and fixed.

If *Style* and *Diction* could be trusted completely, none of these objections would have any force. (Notice, though, that the programs would have to be perfectly accurate. The possibility of error introduces doubt.) Indeed, the programs would become tremendously important teaching tools, because they would indefatigably identify writing errors exactly where the identification does the most good. Can *Style* and *Diction* be improved? IBM has made an important try, a program called *Epistle* (see Dobrin, "What's New"). I have seen *Epistle*, but only at a private demonstration. I was unable to play with it, and I was unable to get precise details about its actual way of working. I did, however, get a good general idea of how it works. At that demonstration, which was held in March 1984, IBM officials announced that the program was in beta (final) test and that it would be released soon. I was skeptical, for the reasons described below. As you read this, if *Epistle* has been released and is widely acclaimed, I might well be wrong.

Epistle improves on the crude analyses done by the *Writer's Workbench* programs by including more fine-grained lists of syntactic labels and adding syntactic indicators of semantic content. Thus *Epistle* might pick out *witch/which* spelling mistakes, because only one is syntactically possible, and it might pass "at that demonstration, which was held in March 1984" because the program correctly analyzes the function of *which* in that sentence (so IBM says). It catches many subject-verb agreement errors, such as "My father eat turkey on Thanksgiving." (This feature, of course, might be useful, because such mistakes are often inadvertent.) To catch such errors, one needs to know a bit about the semantic content of the sentence. IBM has a complicated system of categorizing words, which acts as a formal substitute for knowledge of semantic content. The system might

(I don't know), for instance, identify *eat* as a verb which takes the name of some form of food for its object, and it might also not identify *granite* as food. Then *Epistle* would flag, "My father eats granite on Thanksgiving." *Epistle* also has a complicated user interface that explains (that is, gives textbook definitions of) certain kinds of errors.

Epistle, though, is much like the dog that walks on its hind legs, remarkable, as Johnson said, not because it does it well, but because it does it at all. In the demonstration I saw, the makers claimed that the program caught seventy percent of the errors in "typical business letters." That means, of course, that the garbage ratio was thirty percent and that the program also missed as much as thirty percent of the actual errors. Is that acceptable? No. The same dynamic is at work. The person who is good at grammar doesn't need it; the person who is bad has more garbage to pick through and doesn't have the resources to decide the questionable cases. The online explanations (of Grundian strictness) can't be any more helpful than the grammar book's, even though they are applied to specific sentences, because the student can't be sure if they actually apply. *Epistle* also requires the full attention of an IBM mainframe and takes approximately two minutes per sentence.

A friend of mine at IBM (sorry I have to resort to anonymity, but such are the vagaries of corporate secrecy) only uses *Epistle*'s spelling checker, which, he says, is remarkably good. The usefulness of the program is understandable; many problematic spellings can be resolved by applying a little grammar. Otherwise, *Epistle* is too slow, too inaccurate, and too much of a nuisance to use. It is, I might add, just as much of a distraction as the other programs. It isn't accurate enough to save one much proofreading time. It gives the uninformed exactly the wrong idea about grammar and style. And it wrongly privileges certain kinds of problems – those that can be identified by manipulating syntactic labels.

The problem of distraction is particularly worrisome with *Epistle*, because *Epistle* is meant for the uninformed. As with the *Writer's Workbench*, its simple-mindedness is a feature that's supposed to help sell big computers to large organizations. In such organizations, if my experience is any guide, the program is likely to be imposed rather than used. Writers will be required by harried supervisors to have a Flesch score below 9 and no more than two flags per page. This is a serious form of distraction.

Beyond *Epistle*

But surely, one might say, even if *Epistle* is imperfect, it is one more step in the right direction. Eventually these kinds of programs will be perfected, and then we will have genuine writing aids. One can't say just because *Epistle* doesn't work that writing aids of this type are impossible.

But that is exactly what I do want to say. In saying it, however, I create another problem for my argument, the problem I mentioned right at the beginning. Problem 2: just as it's impossible to say that a tool can never be used, it's impossible to say that a technology can never succeed. I admit that. Any statement of the form "Such and such is impossible" can always be wrong. Nevertheless, it's important to make such statements. We all have limited resources; we all would prefer not to waste them trying to attain unreachable goals. Particularly with technical goals, we should determine whether they can be achieved before we waste time and money trying to achieve them. Witness the current debate about SDI, or perhaps more germane, witness almost all decisions about funding scientific research. Many readers of this paper have delightedly pointed out, "They laughed at the Wright brothers." True, but scarcely a compelling argument. For every new technology that succeeds, thousands more fail.

When should we think a technology will fail? One way is to measure the progress it has made. If, with the tools it has, the technology has traversed much of the distance toward its goal and no barriers remain, optimism is in order. If, however, the technology has not gone very far and has apparently insuperable obstacles before it – if we wish to level the Rocky Mountains with a pickax – then we should be pessimistic. In this particular case, evaluating the tools is relatively simple; the only available tool is syntactic labeling. The problem, therefore, is to measure the size of the remaining obstacles.

Remember that we want a computer that can take any English text and correctly detect in it a significant number of important errors. Leaving aside the problem of deciding which errors, of deciding exactly what counts as an error, of evaluating the purpose and audience of documents, of calibrating how purpose and audience affect the determination of error, of determining which errors are most important, of recommending how the errors can be fixed, of designing an interface, and, of course, of accomplishing all this in a reasonable amount of time – at the very least we have the problem of parsing sentences. One aspect of the problem is the task of parsing prepositional phrases, especially potentially ambiguous prepositional phrases, like those beginning with *in*. Parsing a certain class of sentences, like the following, illustrates the difficulty:

1. The car hit the man in the street.

The sentence can be parsed in two different ways; *in the street* can identify either the man or the location of the accident. For simplicity's sake, let us assume that most English speakers automatically parse the phrase as identifying the location of the hitting. I would like to look for a moment at what we would have to do in order to get the computer to do the same thing. Remember, though, that our method must also allow the computer to parse similar sentences, like the following:

2. The car hit the man in the side.
3. The car hit the man in the tree.
4. The car hit the man in the park.
5. The car hit the man in the play.

Our problem is to structure the syntactic labels so that we obtain the right answer accurately and efficiently. Let us first try the following approach. We will classify the 'nouns' in much the way *Epistle* seems to. For this task, an appropriate classification might be the sort of location they define: location in space (*park, street, tree*), location in the body (*side*), location in activity (*play*), or no location whatsoever. (Most nouns fall into the latter class, for instance, "The car hit the man in the noun.") Such a classification would necessarily be incomplete and ambiguous, but it would be a start. When the computer encounters a preposition like *in*, which takes a location noun as its object, it would immediately consult this list. 'Nouns' which do not identify locations would generate a query. 'Nouns' which do would generate an investigation of other words in the sentence which matched the location noun. (These 'matches' would be contained in another list.) If the list of 'matches' were constructed correctly, then, in sentences 1 and 5, *street* would go with *car* and *play* would go with *man*.

If this list of location nouns looks rather long and difficult to assemble, you're beginning to get the idea. Remember, though, that this method doesn't, by itself, produce an accurate result. The sentence "The car hit the man in the park" could be parsed either way, as associating *park* with the man or as associating it with the car and therefore the location of the hitting. *Side, tree,* and *park* could go with either *car* or *man*. (Imagine the resulting sentences with *man* and *car* reversed to see why straight matches of prepositional phrases and subjects aren't possible.) So we must set up lists of noun-verb conjunctions ('events') which match the objects of the preposition. The idea would be to put *car-hit-man* in a 'traffic accident' category. Since accidents occur in streets and not, generally, in trees, with a little fiddling we can see that *tree* will go with *man* (see Minsky, "Framework"; see Dreyfus for critique).

This list of 'events' would have to be staggeringly large. It would have to be so accurately structured that it would distinguish, for instance, among "The car hit," "The boy hit," "The car passed," and "The boy passed," since each produces a quite different analysis when coupled with the original five prepositional phrases. Would such a structuring take care of our remaining phrases? Perhaps, but it would create a very serious new problem. Let's imagine we have put *car-hit-man* in a 'traffic accident' category, *boy-hit-man* in a 'fight' category, and *car-passed-man* in a 'traffic' category. We had set up these 'event' categories so as to take care of the problem matches. But suddenly the easy matches become stumbling blocks. With the 'traffic' category, we have to rethink the match between *car* and *street*, and with the 'fight' category, we have to rethink the *play* match.

We can't cheat, therefore, and use approximate matches for most situations. We have to match every location noun, as well as every noun-verb construction, with an 'event'. Our already large list is getting bigger and more time-consuming to consult. The list would be more manageable if certain classes of location nouns could be linked with certain types of events. *Side* and *middle* might be grouped together in most 'events' in which a *man* is *hit*, for instance. But in the 'traffic accident' case, "The car hit the man in the middle" can have two quite different meanings – in the middle of the body or the middle of a group of people. So classes of nouns, because they cannot take into account such overlaps, are not allowed, and the lists get bigger. And in fact, we cannot match the nouns alone; we must match them as modified. In a sentence like "The car hit the man in the east side of the parking lot," *in the side* should be parsed in the same way that *in the street* would be. The lists get bigger.

Of course, if we want to preclude failure, we also must take the context into account. If the sentence preceding the original sentence 1 were, "Two men were walking side by side, one on the sidewalk and one in the street," then the parsing of the sentence we had decided on would be incorrect. How big are the lists now?

To begin to get an idea of how big the obstacles are, imagine constructing 'events' which would guarantee the correct parsing of every sentence in this article.

(A note from 1988. This argument is only about the possibility of building a perfectly accurate parser. If you accept the fact that you won't be able to parse ambiguous sentences, you can build a fairly accurate parser. How good the parser would be, of course, depends largely on your ingenuity and the power of your computer. You would have to come up with syntactic clues to sentence structure in a fantastic number of special cases, and you would have to process these in a reasonable amount of time. Linguists at Houghton Mifflin have come up with such a parser, which, as of August 1988, I have seen and tested, though not thoroughly. It is by no means accurate, but it may well be accurate enough and cogent enough for some people to find it helpful – despite the difficulties in using it – mostly, I think, because it catches inadvertent errors, for instance, some subject-verb disagreements.)

A Rescue from Artificial Intelligence?

With the *Writer's Workbench*, an optimist might say, we've come part of the way, and with *Epistle* or the Houghton-Mifflin program we've come even farther. Such an attitude, however, entirely misconstrues the nature of progress in the field. To get a good parser, we saw earlier, the trick is to structure the lists of syntactic labels correctly. An incorrectly structured list, like that assembled by *Diction* or the ones we imagined in our thought experiment, does not constitute progress toward a correctly structured list. It is just one of a million dead-ends. So the existence of any particular incorrectly structured list doesn't mean much as far as the eventual prospects of the field are concerned.

Still, progress does seem to be rapid in at least one sense: the lists have got more complicated very quickly. But the rapidity is illusory. Even though *Writer's Workbench* and *Epistle* have only recently emerged on the public scene, they are relatively old. *Writer's Workbench* was developed along with the rest of the UNIX operating system in the middle and late 1970s. The development effort for *Epistle* dates from 1980.

But even dating the effort from *Writer's Workbench* betrays a serious misunderstanding. The problem of simulating response to meaning has been the most important obstacle for the branch of computer science known as *artificial intelligence* ever since its inception in the 1950s. Three of the classic projects for AI (language translation, speech recognition, and computer vision) require solutions to the meaning problem. None of the projects has been successful; all reported "advances" are merely provisional ways of coping with local problems, not principled solutions.

Have computer scientists been able to make steady progress on any of the standard artificial intelligence problems? By no means (see Dreyfus). Has the advent of larger and faster computers shown that any artificial intelligence problem can be solved? By no means. The research has shown only that the general problem of simulating the understanding of meaning is much bigger than anyone originally thought. People who in the early 1970s made their reputations by claiming that the meaning problem would soon be solved now claim that "soon" means decades or even centuries. Patrick Winston is one such person. He told me, in a discussion of computer programs for writing, that it will be several decades before a solution is even approached. Marvin Minsky told one of my classes that it will take two hundred years.

One important discovery that artificial intelligence has made is that the meaning problem shows up in the most surprising places. You might not think, for instance, that accurate scanning of parts on an assembly line requires a solution to the meaning problem, but it does. It is not surprising that the meaning problem shows up in – and has the same crippling effect on – other kinds of computer writing aids. Invention programs, for instance, require that the program understand the statements of students if they are going to probe ideas and help students build on them in appropriate ways. Template programs (a dutiful offshoot of invention programs for teachers or managers who want to be sure that users get it right) must be able to understand the text so that the template can be modified appropriately. Where either kind of program fails to respond appropriately, it becomes inflexible – more difficult to work with than pencil and paper. Idea processors (outline-structuring programs), too, are inflexible, for the same reason (see Dobrin, "Some Ideas," *Writing*). This fact is by no means obvious; to understand where and how the inflexibility, the lack of responsiveness, creeps in, you have to take the same kind of painful look at the details of these programs' operation as I took at the parsing of "The car hit the man in the street." It is, in fact, a feature of the meaning problem that each simulation of responses to meaning fails in a different way.

Let me return, for a moment, to the Wright brothers. They are often described as having had foresight and vision. But they can equally well be seen as excellent critics. They looked at the state of the currently accepted technology (lighter-than-air craft) and decided it had no future. From our perspective, of course, what they saw looks obvious; all those people flapping their artificial wings were clearly deluded. Why should anyone have believed that those contraptions would work?

I submit that my evaluation of computer aids to writing ought to be equally obvious. Why should anyone think that we can determine what someone means by assembling lists of syntactic labels? Meaning is something humans have invented so that they can help one another cope with life. It arises out of what we are as human beings, our hopes, fears, ideas, experiences, purposes, engagements, involvements. We know the difference between *anticipate* and *expect*, or between hitting a man in the side and hitting him in the tree because, having lived it ourselves, we have a fundamental understanding of what life is like. Why on earth should we believe that understanding of life can be conferred on a machine through long lists of 'nouns' and 'verbs' and 'events'?

When I taught four courses and spent my whole life grading papers carefully, I often felt that my work was simple and mechanical. Would that a machine could do it! But the plain fact is that a machine can't do it. And the reason is simple. When you read a paper, you are responding to the thoughts of another human being. And however limited, painful, obvious, or grammatically capricious those thoughts are, they are yet invested with the fullness and complication of life itself, a fullness and complication which dwarfs all the lists of labels ever assembled.

Does this mean that computers cannot help us? By no means. Computers can still help us whenever we need symbol processing. This simple fact ought to be liberating, not disappointing. It should actually be encouraging. Knowing that we can't effectively write programs that respond to text, we can direct our energies toward more fruitful, more plausible goals. We can make better online editors, better systems for communication, better word processors. That is what I think we should do. After I finished this paper, I discovered I was not alone. I went around the AI department at MIT, and I asked faculty members what kinds of programs would be most useful to students and writers. Here are answers from two noted computer scientists, whom I will let have the last word.

> Better word processors – Joseph Weizenbaum
> Better word processors – Douglas Hofstadter

Notes

[1] Because this article talks about existing programs, it is important to know when the positions it argues were formulated. The arguments were developed in 1983 and first presented in 1984. The article was written in 1986, but some revisions were added in 1988. The revisions are marked.

[2] You can see the difference between *A* and 'A' more clearly if you realize that either can change and leave the other same. When you change typefaces, you change the 'letter' without changing the letter; when you intend it as a transliteration, you change a letter without changing the 'letter'.

[3] The terminology is standard in the philosophy of psychology (see Fodor). Note also that, strictly speaking, the computer does not attach the label, we do (see Haugeland, introduction).

[4] By *perfect*, I mean only that the computer would respond as a reasonably well-

informed person would. People make mistakes, too, but of a different, more reasonable kind. They are mistakes in responding to the meaning of a text.

[5] I was once on a panel with a teacher (who shall remain nameless) who taught *Diction*. Said teacher showed some sample sentences in which *Diction* correctly identified errors. In each case, those sentences could have been fixed better by ignoring the advice of the program, and in each case the teacher failed to notice that.

[6] Lorinda Cherry estimated that the type of each sentence is identified accurately about 86.5% of the time. Her sample, however, was only twenty technical documents. You should, of course, be exactly as skeptical about her claims as you are about claims for other computer programs (see Cherry and Vesterman 10).

[7] Do the uninstructed actually use these programs? In two years of working in the computer rooms at MIT, I have never seen anyone use the *Style* or *Diction* programs.

[8] I know of no other empirical studies of this program. Anecdotal accounts of how the program is used tend to be biased in its favor, as described above.

Local and Global Networking: Implications for the Future

Michael Spitzer

———◆———

W hen the computer was introduced into the classroom, it was viewed as a panacea that, through drill-and-practice software, would transform education. Gradually, the computer has come to be seen as a tool that can support sound pedagogical practices. In composition classes, grammar drills have given way to an emphasis on word processing as a means of improving writing. Countless writers have learned to appreciate the ease with which they can compose and revise with a word processor, and creative teachers have begun to develop effective techniques for encouraging sound composing and revising strategies.

Advances in computer technology now make it possible for computer networks to be used in instruction, but the problem that plagued teachers who were originally attracted to computers now confronts teachers who want to use computers in a networked environment: the courseware that has been developed for most networks is intended primarily for remediation and basic skills instruction (McCroskey 13) – that is, drill and practice once again. Networks are being promoted by vendors because they are easier to administer (programs can be loaded more efficiently, and, because students do not handle disks, problems with stolen, damaged, or illegally copied software can be avoided), and economical (disk drives and printers can be shared among several computers). While these advantages may help make networked computers more attractive, they hardly provide a pedagogical justification for investing in networks. Network vendors and software developers are their own worst enemies when it comes to promoting these products, and teachers should ignore the software while capitalizing on the opportunity inherent in the network itself. Those few teachers fortunate enough to have worked with networked computers are excited by this potential, and it is certain that the technology, still relatively esoteric and not yet widely distributed, will be accepted enthusiastically once this application becomes better known.

Collaboration and Social Construction

The major benefit of a computer network is that it permits computers to talk to each other, allowing users to communicate easily with one another. Computers, which were once thought to promote isolation, may in fact prove to be of greatest help in creating cooperative learning environments. Many teachers who have used computers in a process-based writing classroom have discovered, sometimes serendipitously, that computers promote collaboration. Usually, one student asks a question about how to perform a particular function, and another suggests an answer. Before long, if this sort of cooperation is encouraged rather than stifled, students begin to talk about their writing as well. In an environment in which students write collaboratively, their writing becomes more meaningful to them and their efforts are more productive.

Imaginative teachers have devised numerous assignments to promote collaboration in writing classes with stand-alone computers. As we shall see, networks can foster more systematic collaboration. Students using networks can pool their insights and ideas, engaging in collaborative brainstorming, in writing, with results available to all participants. On a network, students can write to one another; the interaction conveys, with more force than was ever before possible, the idea that writing is a means of communicating.

Written discussion on a computer network, as Trent Batson has noted, changes the social and pedagogical dynamics of a classroom. In a traditional class, the teacher is clearly in command. The students are arrayed in rows, facing the teacher, who controls discussion, directing comments to the class or receiving and redirecting comments from students. On a network, teachers must yield power; their comments have no more prominence than those of the students, and the reduction in authority translates into increased empowerment for students. Group discussion on a network encourages the creation of what Batson calls an "on-line discourse community" that makes it possible for students to move naturally from writing as conversation to more formal modes of writing (32). If knowledge is socially constructed, then an "on-line discourse community" can be a powerful tool in the process of creating a community of knowledgeable and skilled writers. Whether the students all work in the same classroom or send messages across the country, the social context of the network provides them with an immediate audience, one concerned not simply with "correcting" their papers, and their writing can assume a purpose that is recognizable to them. Because they can change the social dynamic of a classroom and also provide student writers with a genuine and uncontrived audience, networks have the potential to transform student writing from listless academic drudgery into writing that is purposeful and reader-based.

The Range of Networking Technology

Students who write on a network can participate in collaborative environments not duplicable in any other way, and the network can provide students with resources that would not otherwise be available. With a network, students sitting at different machines can share an electronic workspace, conduct a discussion in writing, compose or revise one text collaboratively and simultaneously. By combining collaborative writing strategies with computer-based writing techniques, teachers have the opportunity to link two powerful currents in writing instruction. For example, in a typical revision exercise in a regular classroom, or even in a computer classroom, students are presented with a passage that needs improvement. The students can discuss the passage and then, either individually or in groups, work at making changes. In a networked classroom, the passage to be revised can be broadcast to the screen of every student in the class. After reading the passage, the students can discuss the text – in writing – and work on revising it. Their individual revisions can then be discussed (again, in writing, if desired) either by small groups or by the whole class. The written work is available instantly for all to see, and transcripts of the written discussion can be printed out for later reference.

When students write to one another rather than to their teachers, the quality of their writing tends to improve. Speaking about basic writers, Sirc observed:

> [C]ollaboration and the constant expression of ideas in writing paid off for many students in the quality of both their papers and their comments on the network. The saturation in writing and thinking about writing afforded by this network did much to nurture my students' sense of themselves as writers. (103)

Another researcher found that students take greater care when they write to their peers than they do when they write for their professors (Bork 71). Furthermore, the enthusiasm generated by computer collaboration carries over into all aspects of a writing course:

> [S]tudents were indeed accumulating an impressive repertoire of writing strategies, many of them learned from each other. But perhaps most important was the sense of commitment and collaboration generated in our community of correspondents. One student compared the atmosphere of corresponding in our class with the peer critiquing in her studio art classes. (Skubikowski and Elder 201)

Sirc's students collaborated on a fairly sophisticated local area network; Skubikowski and Elder's students communicated through the college's mainframe machine. The computer networks used for writing can be of several kinds, and can be either local or distant. While all networks share certain characteristics, the specific features of a given network help determine how it can be used as well as its overall effectiveness as a tool for collaborative writing.

Local Area Networks

A local area network consists of a group of microcomputers linked to one another electronically. Such a network is usually controlled by a single computer equipped with a hard-disk drive. The other computers in the network access software or word-processing files stored in this computer's memory. One of several available "chat" facilities can be incorporated into the network to enable synchronous communication in writing to take place. With such a network, students can collaborate in the creation of a text, comment on one another's texts, and give each other feedback about their writing at the time the writing occurs, without having to leave their seats.

Mainframe Networking

Many of the benefits of a local area network can be realized by using a mainframe computer, which, in effect, functions as a file server for a number of terminals. One difference between these two technologies is that the networked microcomputers can work independently if the file server should malfunction. With a mainframe, if the computer goes down, none of the terminals can be used. (Microcomputers can also be connected to the mainframe, in which case they can function independently should the mainframe malfunction.) There is also a wider range of writing software available for microcomputers than for mainframes, and the word-processing programs are generally less cumbersome and easier to master than the text editors available on mainframes, particularly for students who lack experience with large computers.

Computer Conferencing

A computer conference is similar to a local area network in the sense that it connects several different microcomputers to one another. It differs in that instead of using a microcomputer as a file server, it uses a mainframe to store shared information. Computers can be hardwired directly to the mainframe, or they can be connected through a modem and telephone lines. If the telephone is used, the connection can be made to a computer down the street, across town, or anywhere in the world. Special telephone services, such as Telenet and Tymnet, make long-distance conferencing convenient. The conferencing software permits users to organize written messages into discussion topics that are accessible to many users.[1]

Plain Vanilla Conferencing

In the absence of a full-fledged network, electronic mail and bulletin boards can be used for a rudimentary form of electronic communication. At Utah State University, for example, Joyce Kinkead and her colleagues use electronic mail to "build discourse communities" (338). Under the leadership of Al Rogers, the San Diego School Networking Project has devised a relatively inexpensive method of linking students through a long-distance network. Essentially an electronic mail system, the San Diego project uses an Apple-based bulletin board. In this network, no student writing is done online. No dedicated phone lines are needed, nor do students need access to modems. Classroom writing activities take place on school computers during the day, and material is transmitted to the network late at night (Rogers and Miller-Souviney 4–7). (The computer can be set up to transmit and receive information by itself, without any direct human involvement.) This electronic conference lacks many of the features of more sophisticated networks, but it does allow students to correspond electronically with peers in other locations.

An even simpler system has been devised by Helen Schwartz for *Seen*, a software program for character analysis in literature. One component of the program consists of a bulletin board to which students post analytic remarks for comment and feedback from other students (48).

Collaborative Activities for Students

While we can wax eloquent about the virtues and wonders of the technology, it is important to remember that our purpose in using networked computers is to improve writing. Fortunately, the changes in writing habits and practices that the technology makes possible are precisely those changes we want to encourage in our students. Collaborative writing on the computer makes writing more enjoyable, extends students' willingness to spend time writing, enlarges their awareness of audience, makes it easier for them to face the blank screen, clarifies the need for revision, and facilitates revising. Students can learn that their peers have experiences similar to their own and that these experiences can be discussed with, and illuminated by, others. Collaboration thus can help produce a self-reflective attitude (whose absence is often a major weakness among student writers), and encourage students to attend to the needs of a real audience (see Batson; Peyton and Michaelson; Sirc; Skubikowski and Elder; Thompson).

Teacher Intervention and Modeling

A major advantage of having students work on a network is that the teacher has the opportunity to intervene directly during the writing process. In most writing classes, students write papers, then submit them to the teacher for comments and grades. By the time the papers are returned, the students have lost interest or must turn their attention to the next assignment. If the students are writing in a networked environment, the teacher can intervene while the text is being created, when students are most receptive to advice and when that advice can do the most good because it can be adopted and applied instantly. This approach to instruction – used by teachers of swimming, tennis, music performance, and (as the student cited earlier noted) studio art – makes much more sense than does the prevailing writing-instruction approach of collecting drafts and returning them later.

While intervention during the writing process is possible in any computer writing class, the network permits the instructor to intervene on the student's individual screen, and makes the process easier and more direct. In a networked classroom, the instructor can model global revision strategies so that they appear directly on each student's screen. Research has shown that students tend to avoid such global revision when left to their own devices (see, e.g., Collier; Harris; Hawisher, "Effects"), probably because they don't understand what teachers mean when they speak of "developing ideas." The students may know the commands needed to move or insert blocks of text but do not understand the reasons for using these commands. The use of a network to show revision as it occurs may prove to be the most effective method of explaining and demonstrating the process. For example, a teacher using a network can take a paragraph from a student's text in progress and present it on every screen in the class. Then, working with the entire class, the teacher can show how a statement can be expanded into an argument. Working together, the class can decide what supporting details are needed to buttress the argument and where they can best be added.

When teachers show students where and when to use the features of the word processor that expert writers take for granted but that novice writers ignore or misapply, students learn how to use the computer to improve their writing. Diane Thompson reports:

> Very few of my students have ever spent much time doing extensive revision, although all of them, when pressed, can explain what revision ought to be. [The network] allows me to walk students through the revision process, discussing the hows and whys of each change as they watch it being made. After students have participated in two or three of these dynamic revision sessions, they become comfortable using the power of the computer to make significant revisions in their writing, not just surface corrections. (96)

The Teacher as Coach

A significant change in the relationship between teacher and students occurs when the teacher comments on texts as they are being composed instead of after they have been written. Instead of being a judge, the teacher functions more like a coach or an editor, someone who makes suggestions, asks for clarification, and gives encouragement. In addition, the teacher serves, again, as a model whose own writing is visible to the students. The effect of these changes is to turn the writing classroom into a virtual electronic workshop.

In such a workshop, teachers can orchestrate a variety of simultaneous activities that put students in control of their own learning and create collaborative environments advocated by writers such as Bruffee ("Collaborative Learning") and Elbow. The value of these activities was endorsed by George Hillocks, who argues that by far the most successful mode of writing instruction incorporates a high degree of peer interaction among students (*Research* 122). In a networked classroom, some students can work individually on their composing or revising, while others work in network-supported electronic peer groups for review of a given text or the texts of groups of students. Yet another group of students can engage in cooperative prewriting activities.

Networked computers may, in fact, prove most valuable for students during prewriting, when they can collaborate in brainstorming or other creative strategies. It is possible, of course, for students to brainstorm together in a conventional classroom, and hardly a writing teacher exists who has not written, on a chalkboard, lists of ideas that students generate collaboratively. While this classroom exercise shows students what they can accomplish when they work together, it is teacher-directed and requires students to take notes in order to benefit fully. If, however, the brainstorming takes place through a network, students can manipulate text and rearrange ideas together. In a traditional classroom, students have to shift gears to move from verbal discussion to written discourse; on a network, they do all the preliminary work in writing and thus no shift is needed. When the brainstorming session is over, each student has access to a printed record of the shared experience; some networks allow each student to save the session on a word-processing file and then use the file as the basis for writing a draft, either collaboratively or individually.

Student Creativity and Responsiveness

Distant networks and computer conferencing also offer opportunities to enrich the writing of students by affording them audiences of their peers and an authentic sense of purpose. Teachers have often encouraged students to develop pen pals as a means of corresponding, say, with people their own age and of exploring other cultures. But the exchange of letters is slow and student enthusiasm for the activity often wilts as the time lag between letters grows. Betsy Bowen and Jeffrey Schwartz, in a project connected to the Bread Loaf School of English, report on an experiment in which high school students in a suburb of Pittsburgh communicate regularly with one group of students on an Indian reservation in South Dakota and another group of students living in a small farming community in Montana. Using conferencing, the students write to one another regularly and receive responses within a day or two. The students' enthusiasm has not waned, according to their teachers. Elementary school students in Glen Cove, New York, participated in a similar experiment, called Star Link, except that they communicated with their peers in a school in Australia. The San Diego School Networking Project, mentioned earlier, uses a computer bulletin board to link students in different communities. With nodes in Nebraska, Pennsylvania, New York, New Hampshire, Connecticut, and other locations, the San Diego project is structured to promote communication among students with different backgrounds and interests. Each participating class is encouraged to prepare a class biography and set up a class newspaper. Students are organized into teams of correspondents who write news dispatches about school activities, local news, and national events that relate to kids and schools. A student editorial board reviews all articles, returns them for rewriting when necessary, edits as needed, and finally, selects dispatches to be sent to the bulletin board. Dispatches from other schools are downloaded to be read by the participating class (Rogers and Miller-Souviney 6-7). At Middlebury College, Kathleen Skubikowski and John Elder used a conferencing technique to have students respond electronically to the journal entries of classmates. The experience generated excitement and commitment among the students that delighted their teachers (199). Perhaps the success of these experiments is the result, in part, of their novelty, but it appears that the immediacy of response and feedback is equally important.

Student writing in these computer conference projects should be markedly different from the writing produced by students for their teachers. In 1975, James Britton and his colleagues studied two thousand pieces of writing by high school students and concluded that up to eighty-four percent was "transactional"–that is, intended to inform or persuade – rather than expressive, a mode more congenial and helpful to students learning to write (Martin 26–27). This statistical breakdown is misleading, I think, because when students write assignments for school, generally, their chief purpose is to demonstrate mastery of a subject to their teachers. The primary exception to this practice occurs in writing classes, in which rhetorical modes such as persuasive essays are assigned.

Even in writing classes, the situation is artificial: the only purpose students have for writing is that they are required to do so, and they write for a captive audience, the teacher. Students do not have to determine who their readers will be, how much or how little their readers will know about their subject, or how to provide information and organize it so that it is useful to their readers. But when these same students write to other students in their class, or to students in another town or in another part of the country, they must consider such questions as: What are my readers like? What do they know about my subject? What do I have to tell them so they will understand my point? In other words, participating in networks provides students with a focus and sense of purpose that are absent in most academic writing. Instead of writing for their teachers, they write *to one another.*

An Electronic Library

A network can provide students with other resources that are helpful to writers. The file server might contain a database of information relevant to a particular topic or to several topics. Students in need of information about the topic can summon up files from the database – either commercially available or prepared specifically by the teacher for a given assignment – then transfer that information into their own word-processing files. This activity can take place whenever needed, allowing students to obtain help as they are writing, without having to leave their texts to go to the library. When reference material is accessible in this way, research becomes an integral part of the writing process rather than an arbitrarily assigned task. Just as a teacher's comment is most helpful during composing, resource material is most beneficial if it is available when needed.

Mainframe computers and distant networks provide students with the same research resources as local area networks. In fact, these networks offer the additional advantage of being available at all times and of being accessible via modem from any location. Generally speaking, local area networks function best when all participants use the network simultaneously. For distance networks, the same is not the case, since the host computer stores all data until it is called for, and the data are available to users so long as the host computer is operational. Distance networks, therefore, are not restricted to users who must be present in the same place at the same time, and have particular appeal for asynchronous use.

Professional Collaboration

The versatility of networked computers as tools of communication can enhance the roles of teachers as researchers, writers, and members of the profession. Computer networks help make collaboration on articles quick and easy. Colleagues find that earlier methods of collaboration in which they prepared drafts on their individual computers and then exchanged printouts have become as tedious and outdated as writing a draft by hand and then typing final copies with carbon paper. And just as networks help break down the isolation of students in a classroom, networking offers teachers a window to the outside world, allowing them to keep abreast of developments in the profession. Finally, networking provides an electronic sounding board, through which teachers can voice their concerns about troublesome issues to a sympathetic audience of colleagues.

Overcoming Incompatibility

Distance networks eliminate many of the obstacles of time, place, and circumstance that inhibit collaboration among professionals. Such networks even overcome the problems that arise when collaborators have incompatible computers. In computer conferencing, a Macintosh computer can communicate with an IBM or compatible machine, or with an Apple IIE or a DEC Rainbow. Consequently, users can collaborate with one another who would not otherwise have the opportunity. For example, if two members of my department decided to collaborate on an article but had different microcomputers, each would have to write a draft of the article, or of an assigned portion of it, print it out, and give the printout to the collaborator for comment and editing. They would have to send the printouts to each other by mail or meet in person to exchange portions of the text. Many of the advantages of using computers would be lost in the process and, ultimately, one of the collaborators would have to retype the text of the other so that the final document was prepared and formatted on the same word processing package. Bernhardt and Appleby note that several of the respondents to their survey cited problems caused by incompatible computers as a limitation on their attempts to write collaboratively (31).

With the availability of a computer conference, all of these roadblocks can be overcome. For example, until recently I did most of my writing on an Apple IIE, while a colleague used an AT&T 6300. We worked together on a grant proposal, but since we could not simply exchange disks, we decided to use our college's computer conferencing facility for our collaborative writing task. I wrote a draft of the proposal and uploaded the file to a conference in the college's host computer. My colleague, who lives about fifty miles away, then dialed the computer, downloaded my draft into a word-processing file on his AT&T, and began immediately to revise. Within a few hours, he transmitted his revision to the college computer; I downloaded it and made additional changes. Before we were finished, we sent one another numerous drafts, and, working together for two days, we produced a proposal that was as good as we could make it. Had we used a more traditional method of exchanging texts, we could never have finished so quickly, and we would have had to settle for a less successful product.

On another proposal, I collaborated with colleagues at three other institutions, each in a different state. While it might have been possible for a single author to write the proposal and perhaps get back a set of comments from each of the other writers, we could not have produced a truly collaborative effort had we not used the computer conferencing system. One person was the principal author, but he received important feedback and assistance throughout the writing process. In particular, he benefited from an immediate audience response, and sections of the text prompted comments that led to the inclusion of new material, new strategies, and a revised sense of purpose.

A Forum for Debate and Exchange

Computer conferencing lends itself not only to short-term collaboration but also to long-term discussion of specific topics, issues, and concerns. The Exxon Education Foundation, for instance, has funded a computer conference for college English teachers throughout the country, and more than seventy participants from over thirty states engage in discussion on how better to use computers to teach writing. Participants find that they can keep current on various research activities, exchange information on new software programs and teaching strategies, and help one another learn about new topics, such as artificial intelligence. Colleagues have debated the value of all software besides word processing, investigated and speculated about the process of invention, and contemplated collaborative studies on the effects of word processing on student writing. A partial list of conference titles can give some sense of the range of discussion: Teach, Research, Using *Writer's Workbench*, Exercise Exchange, Artificial Intelligence, Lab Setups, and Tech Teach are a few of the branch conferences that emerged. Several members of the conference have experimented with synchronous brainstorming sessions, and some have written papers collaboratively using the conference – from conception to final draft. It is difficult to capture the flavor of these exchanges by quoting excerpts, because the quotes distort the context, and when respondents become involved in a topic, they tend to write lengthy notes. Nevertheless, the following notes, in response to a comment about a study that found that word processing did not help students revise more effectively, can provide some idea of the exchanges possible:

> DRODRIGUES: . . . I think we may have to realize that if students don't have a
> good notion of what a fine product looks like, no way of producing their text will

help them. The old reading-writing connection explains the problem.
Not having read enough, they haven't internalized what a text should look like.

MSOUTHWELL: It is confirmed by both my experience and my reading that word processing is generally not found to make a difference per se in quality of writing. What it does do, however, is permit a revision of curricular strategies, so that activities which can improve the quality of writing can be used. . . .

TCOLLINS: The article . . . confirms some of the earlier studies by Bridwell and Sirc on revision, quality, and advanced writers.
We may look in the wrong place if we expect word processing to have a dramatic impact on the texture of student writing and gross aspects of their process, especially if the study is done in an early stage of the students' use of the computer. (Why should reliable habits change?)

DFLETCHER: In terms of revision, is this really possible unless the writer is willing to rethink a prior position or stance, dig into primary or secondary sources, or accept the notion that what is initially stated might not yet be adequate or complete?

TJENNINGS: Revision isn't the important thing. As Dawn [Rodrigues] said before, what matters is that writers perceive – register – actually "internalize" the desire to change what is already on the page. And that desire . . . has to involve a purpose more personal than just "to please the teacher" or "to pass the course." Hooray for revising, but let's let it happen – rather than teach people that they must.[2]

In computer conferencing, researchers gain the same advantages from collaboration that students achieve using local area networks. They gain psychological support from the knowledge that others are grappling with the same kinds of problems that they face, and they derive a sense of community from the fact that, although they may feel isolated on their own campuses, other researchers at other institutions share their interests. In addition, professionals develop a renewed sense of commitment to their scholarly pursuits because they can communicate regularly with peers. Conference members are generally enthusiastic about the level of discussion and the immediacy of response they receive. Here is one comment:

> I can't believe how much discussion and sharing of perspectives was generated by my initial statement of concern over Gail Hawisher's article in *RTE*. And to have Gail herself join in the discussion. . . . Wow! There are some wonderful people here: intelligent, insightful, concerned, and way out in front when it comes to computers and composition. (Golub)

Other professional uses of computer conferencing are also possible. The New York Institute of Technology conferencing facility is home to an electronic writer's net-workshop. Authors submit manuscripts in progress for critical discussion by other professional writers and receive thoughtful and speedy responses to their work. Another series of conferences is sponsored by the New York State Education Department for teachers and administrators throughout the state. These conferences afford ready access to a large number of knowledgeable people and cover a wide range of topics, from the application of software in a specific discipline, to teacher training, to ways of preventing students from dropping out of school. By providing a place to brainstorm and explore ideas, the conferences are a time-saving resource; they are also a source of psychological support from sympathetic peers.

For all its positive attributes, computer conferencing is a new mode of communication, one whose conventions take some getting used to. Because conferencing uses text on a screen, it seems familiar, but it is clearly a new kind of text, more fluid and temporary than print, and different too from a word-processing file, which is, after all, print in progress. (See Spitzer, "Writing Style," for a discussion of the special characteristics of computer conferencing as a medium.) Once users become familiar with conferencing, however, they discover that it can become a powerful medium for collaboration and the exchange of information.

Today, when the majority of writing teachers still do not use computers in their classrooms, an essay that anticipates a time when students will work in writing classrooms equipped with networked computers linked to large databases and classes in other schools, and writing teachers will collaborate electronically with colleagues throughout the country, may seem esoteric, far-fetched, and foolhardy. The development of networks for teachers and students just since 1984, however, suggests that those people who have been introduced to networking and its advantages have recognized its potential and the benefits it offers.

In 1984, in fact, few of the networking projects described in this article existed. Those that I have mentioned are growing, and other network-based projects are being started or expanded. For example, in 1985 Trent Batson of Gallaudet University designed a local area networking environment called ENFI, and several other colleges have since adopted the instructional approach it represents (Batson 32). Early in 1987, officials in the New York State Education Department began to encourage writing networks for students within school districts and from district to district within the state (Kidder). At Pennsylvania State University, an online editor-coach helps composition students in a local high school (Tamplin).

The originators of these pioneering networking activities have had to cope with technical problems and the associated frustrations that inevitably accompany the introduction of a new technology. That they persisted is a tribute both to their perseverance and to their confidence that the activity was worth the investment of time, effort, and money. If the development of computers in general can serve as a model, then networks will undoubtedly become easier to use and require less technical know-how to implement as the technology becomes more widespread. The cost of microcomputers keeps going down, and the number of computers available in schools keeps going up. Within a few years, networked computer-writing classrooms will become commonplace.

In the future, writing classes will be able to take advantage of databases stored on hard-disk drives or mainframe computers, will have the capacity for electronic messaging among students and between teachers and students, will open the walls of the classroom to other groups of writers in other localities, and will permit collaborative invention and cooperative composing and revising. None of these activities will by themselves teach students to write better. They will, however, provide an environment in which writing is a fluid and dynamic process; communication is an important, integral part of the writing class; and students are motivated to help themselves and others express their ideas clearly and forcefully.

Behind all the razzle-dazzle of the technology lies the fact that networking provides the means for improved communication in writing. Put another way, networking helps transform writing into communication. As more and more teachers become aware of the benefits that networking provides, they will embrace this application of technology as a means of collaborating with their colleagues and helping their students write better.

Notes

[1] For a fuller discussion of how computer conferencing works, see Spitzer, "Computer Conferencing," and Feenberg.

[2] These notes, by Dawn Rodrigues, Michael Southwell, Terence Collins, David Fletcher, and Ted Jennings, were all sent to Fifth C.

Reading and Writing Connections: Composition Pedagogy and Word Processing

Gail E. Hawisher

Although English teachers often greet both in-service training and computers with resistance and resentment, an ability to work with microcomputers as tools for learning and teaching seems increasingly important. With the advent of the first fully assembled microcomputer during the late 1970s, technology has indeed become a part of the school setting. For a while it appeared that this new technology might remain in the hands of science and math teachers – or perhaps spread to vocational and business departments, where students would be taught word processing and spreadsheet applications in preparation for the world of work. But as microcomputers made their way into public schools in the early 1980s, they also became tools for teaching composition. Indeed, the proliferation of software advertised in catalogs indicates an already large and growing market for language arts courseware. To mention *HBJ Writer*, William Wresch's *Writer's Helper*, or Science Research Associate's *Electronic Ink* is only to touch on a few of the integrated word-processing packages that have been designed especially for schools. Other programs such as style checkers, vocabulary builders, heuristic and invention software, and workbook-like drill-and-practice options suggest a multitude of ways computers are being used in English curricula. In addition, a catalog from the National Council of Teachers of English lists five books, published since 1983 by the council, devoted solely to computer applications. (See Standiford, Jaycox, and Auten; Wresch, *Computer*; Parson; Selfe, *Computer-Assisted Instruction*; Rodrigues and Rodrigues.)

Microcomputers present a special challenge for English teachers and teacher educators. As teachers, we must decide whether we should develop the necessary skills to teach with computers, whether the technology is useful for working with students, and, if it is, what strategies prove effective. Those of us who are teacher educators must consider these issues in addition to determining productive methods for introducing computers to teachers. Furthermore, in collaboration with teachers, teacher educators need to develop strategies that build upon good process-centered curricula – and try to construct models for using computers that improve current pedagogy for composition instruction. We have, then, not one goal to accomplish but three: (1) to keep abreast of current developments in hardware and software applicable to writing; (2) to be informed of new issues in composition theory and pedagogy that might lend themselves to computer writing; (3) to design and implement innovative strategies for introducing teachers to trends in both composition and computers. In this way, computers-and-writing pedagogy can encompass what we have learned from the past as we familiarize ourselves with the technology that is becoming integral to English curricula.

The model presented here is based on an approach for introducing composition pedagogy and word processing to English teachers that was developed for a weekend semester course and a four-week summer workshop at the University of Illinois.[1] It recommends teaching strategies emphasizing connections between reading and writing that secondary teachers themselves can use with their students. After the approach and context are described, the reactions of teachers to both the workshop and computers will be discussed, along with their evaluation of the experience as a whole. Also explored are some promising as well as disturbing developments that occurred when teachers returned to their schools. The overall purpose of this essay is to set forth a model for introducing computers to English teachers and to invite further discussion and inquiry into effective training through in-service efforts.

Conceptual Framework of the Model

According to JoAnne Vacca and Anthony Manna, in-service workshops seem to have the greatest chance for success when they are planned jointly by classroom teachers and teacher educators. Recognizing the wisdom of this advice, a group of us – a mixture of teachers and teacher educators – developed a curriculum to engage participants in testing the value of computers for themselves and for their students while, at the same time, learning strategies that combined a process approach to writing instruction with an emphasis on reading and writing connections.

The philosophy underlying the model is that computers are most effective in a writing curriculum when teachers and students use them to write – that is, instead of supporting a workbook structure of dull exercises, computers should be used creatively as writing tools. A problem that often confronts English teachers is what courseware to choose for their students. Instead of asking teachers to deal with such choices early on, the model presents the computer as a writing tool rather than as a teaching tool. Teachers are asked to judge its merit for their own writing, not to assess a huge array of instructional software. An assumption supporting this model is that teachers must first evaluate word processing for their writing before they can introduce it to students. Since composing is regarded as a way of learning (Emig, "Writing"), the computer is also seen as a facilitator of learning – not as a delivery system for instruction. Thus workshop participants are taught word processing with an eye toward teaching students to capitalize on any advantages in using the technology for learning and for writing.

The in-service model, then, is built on a workshop format in which teachers not only learn about writing on a computer but also write extensively, and the topic of their written assignments – the content for the course – is composition instruction. In addition, the teaching strategies are grounded in theory that encourages close analytical reading as one basis for writing. Lester Faigley, in "Competing Theories of Process," has labeled this process-centered perspective the "social view," a conception perhaps most fully articulated by Patricia Bizzell. Bizzell stresses the need for students to practice academic genres if they are to become successful writers in college. David Bartholomae, similarly, argues that students "must appropriate . . . a specialized discourse, and they have to do this as though they [are] easily and comfortably one with their audience, as though they [are] members of the academy . . . " (4–5). Thus students should learn how to think and write in ways that are acceptable to other members of a particular "rhetorical community" if they are to become insiders of that group. For the college-bound, a rhetorical community may include writers who engage in academic writing, a category that becomes more specialized when we consider the writing conventions of particular disciplines – that is, subcultures of a larger rhetorical community; or it may include members of the student's future vocation or profession, whose texts likewise are characterized by certain ways of thinking and by specific conventions of usage that Bartholomae terms "commonplaces." Rhetorical communities, according to this view, are recognized by their adherence to the textual norms of a particular culture, whether it is science, law, social work, or education, all subcultures of the larger rhetorical community of writers within the United States.

An assumption underlying a writing-from-sources pedagogy associated with the social perspective is that the rhetorical conventions of a community can be learned by a close study of its texts. To help students internalize and assess critically characteristics of writing in particular discourse communities, we can teach them to read analytically, marking text as they go, and to summarize, synthesizing another writer's ideas through the process of writing. Students are then encouraged to examine critically the ideas and structure of particular texts, perhaps by listing patterns of language, to help them determine the content and form that the writer has chosen as a way of creating meaning (Axelrod and Cooper 1–31). As these strategies have made their way into college-writing instruction for both basic and competent writers, several members of our profession have described innovative methods for capitalizing on reading and writing connections (see Spatt; Jacobus; Bazerman, *Informed Writer*; Gunner and Frankel). Moreover, in research exploring the reading processes and writing products of college students using sources, Mary Lynch Kennedy found that the more able writers in her study read and reread with pencils in hand, making notes as they progressed. Their writing also seemed to show a constructive use of their notes. Thus students – in both high school and college – can be encouraged to use reading effectively in their writing by practicing techniques that proficient readers and writers employ.

Intrinsic to the model, then, is the belief that if teachers are taught theory and pedagogy relating to computers with techniques grounded in the social view of writing, they can evaluate such strategies for their own classrooms. This theoretical perspective of writing pedagogy is at the heart of the instruction advocated in the workshop approach presented here.

Throughout the workshop, teachers are asked to judge the worth of computers in light of current research and theory regarding the technology as well as the reading and writing strategies associated with composing processes. To this end, a collection of readings are assembled that focus on the following: writing as process, reading as process, research and theory in written composition, and research in word processing. A sampling of possible readings includes the following articles: Donald Murray, "Teach Writing as Process Not Product"; Linda Flower and John Hayes, "A Cognitive Process Theory of Writing"; George Hillocks, "What Works in Teaching Composition"; Robert Tierney, "Writer-Reader Transactions"; Charles Bazerman, "A Relationship between Reading and Writing"; and Lester Faigley, "Competing Theories of Process." Some possible articles for inclusion that relate specifically to computers and composition are Donald Ross and Lillian Bridwell, "Computer-Aided Composing"; Kathleen Kiefer, "Writing: Using the Computer as Tool"; William Costanzo, "Language, Thinking, and the Culture of Computers"; Bertram Bruce, Sarah Michaels, and Karen Watson-Gegeo, "How Computers Can Change the Writing Process"; and Stephen Marcus, "Computers and English." (See the "Works Cited" section for other names listed in fig. 1.)

As a result of their readings and experience with word processing, teachers should begin to wonder how, if at all, computers fit into a conceptual framework of a writing curriculum. And, teachers may ask, if computers are to be adjuncts to the teaching of writing, how can they be incorporated into a methodology that proves profitable for composition instruction? Are there other ways computers and word processing can be used that go beyond what we know about teaching writing in conventional classrooms? These, then, are the conceptual and practical concerns that should guide the workshops for secondary and college English teachers of writing.

A Description of the Model

Based on these concerns, the in-service model in Fig. 1 presents the goals of the workshop, the conceptual underpinnings of the training, and the methodology used.

The vertical column of boxes at the left outlines the goals of the course, primarily those of helping teachers to understand writing as process, to familiarize themselves with theory and research in both composition and computers, and to determine whether computers might be appropriate in the context of their own

Figure 1. An In-Service Model for Introducing Word-Processing and Composition Pedagogy to English Teachers

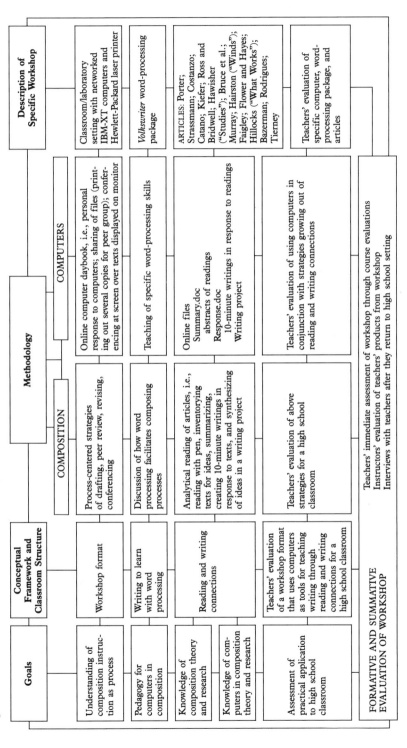

Goals	Conceptual Framework and Classroom Structure	Methodology			Description of Specific Workshop
			COMPOSITION	COMPUTERS	
Understanding of composition instruction as process	Workshop format	Process-centered strategies of drafting, peer review, revising, conferencing		Online computer daybook, i.e., personal response to computers; sharing of files (printing out several copies for peer group); conferencing at screen over texts displayed on monitor	Classroom/laboratory setting with networked IBM-XT computers and Hewlett-Packard laser printer
Pedagogy for computers in composition	Writing to learn with word processing	Discussion of how word processing facilitates composing processes		Teaching of specific word-processing skills	*Volkswriter* word-processing package
Knowledge of composition theory and research	Reading and writing connections	Analytical reading of articles, i.e., reading with pen, inventorying texts for ideas, summarizing, creating 10-minute writings in response to texts, and synthesizing of ideas in a writing project		Online files Summary.doc abstracts of readings Response.doc 10-minute writings in response to readings Writing project	ARTICLES: Porter; Strassmann; Costanzo; Catano; Kiefer; Ross and Bridwell; Hawisher ("Studies"); Bruce et al.; Murray; Hairston ("Winds"); Faigley; Flower and Hayes; Hillocks ("What Works"); Bazerman; Rodrigues; Tierney
Knowledge of computers in composition theory and research					
Assessment of practical application to high school classroom	Teachers' evaluation of a workshop format that uses computers as tools for teaching writing through reading and writing connections for a high school classroom	Teachers' evaluation of above strategies for a high school classroom		Teachers' evaluation of using computers in conjunction with strategies growing out of reading and writing connections	Teachers' evaluation of specific computer, word-processing package, and articles

FORMATIVE AND SUMMATIVE EVALUATION OF WORKSHOP

Teachers' immediate assessment of workshop through course evaluations
Instructors' evaluation of teachers' products from workshop
Interviews with teachers after they return to high school setting

classrooms. Rather than merely to provide instructional strategies, our aim was to explore theory and research that might inform practice after the workshop ended. When in the future, for example, bibliographical information and other resources become available on computers in English classrooms, teachers would be able, if they chose, to use such databases as material to complement what Hillocks has called the "environmental mode" of teaching (*Research*). Teachers would build on what they had learned as technology transforms the teaching of English composition.

The second column of boxes, under the heading "Conceptual Framework and Classroom Structure," presents the context and philosophical underpinnings that should guide teaching strategies. It recommends a workshop format that models process-centered techniques (described in the third column of boxes, under "Methodology") and suggests ways teachers might use reading, writing, and word processing with their students. In the workshop format, students collaborate on projects, commenting on classmates' writing displayed on the computer screen before them, and then share ideas that come from these sessions with the rest of the class. In addition, the format is based on the notion that writing is a learning process – that as students write, they explore how new concepts support or contradict ideas they have already assimilated. In networked computer environments, furthermore, students can immediately retrieve and respond to their classmates' texts, thus incorporating others' ideas in their own writing – an interaction that should stimulate creativity and responsiveness to the reader. Students, in this way, can encounter the notion of "intertext" through what James Porter has termed the "pedagogy of intertextuality." That is, students read and analyze the writing of other members of a community and come to realize that "every text admitted into a discourse community changes the constitution of the community" (41). In a networked classroom of their peers, the standards and conventions of a community are those that students themselves have established through their writings. Thus, by examining the discursive practices of the members of their class, as well as of other rhetorical communities, students can discover how writers influence each other.

In the third and fourth columns, under "Methodology," a series of boxes describes the role of word processing in this model of composition instruction. Teachers keep three online files to record their personal reactions to writing with word processing (the computer daybook), their responses to the readings (response.doc), and abstracts of their readings (summary.doc). Using word processing and the reading and writing strategies featured in the workshop, they develop a writing project based on their interests and readings for the in-service program. Essentially, the daybook contains expressive writings that are meant for their eyes alone, unless they choose to share their entries with others. Their response file, similarly, contains personal reactions to the readings; often these responses become sources for more public writings and are worked into expository and persuasive texts. These files, along with another containing summaries of readings for the course, all contribute to the writing project. For the writing project, participants take a concept encountered in the course (such as intertextuality, revision, or collaborative learning) and, using readings along with selected colleagues' writings, explore how the concept might be applied in a computer-writing class for their students. In addition to demonstrating writing-from-sources techniques (e.g., reading with pen, inventorying texts for ideas, summarizing readings, and synthesizing ideas from several readings), the activity was designed to illustrate how computers can facilitate the bringing together of the various aims of discourse – expressive, referential, and persuasive – to enhance students' writing. Teachers were thus able to judge the efficacy of practicing reading and writing strategies and applying them to composition instruction with the aid of word processing.

Finally, the series of boxes at the right includes the specific hardware, software, and readings that essentially are the content for the workshop, although other content might be easily substituted. In fact, the flexibility of content is one of the strengths of the model in that teachers are presented with a scheme they can adapt to their own classes by introducing appropriate subject matter. These particular readings were selected to acquaint participants with the most recent writings in composition and computers, a selection that needs to be brought up to date each year.

Undergirding the model at two levels is evaluation. The next-to-last horizontal series of boxes calls for teachers to evaluate the worth of what they are learning while they are learning it. In other words, they judge whether the reading and writing strategies combined with word processing would work for their students. For our particular group, teachers volunteered statements such as, "This might not work like this, but if I also used my method of doing it this way, I think it would have a chance of succeeding with students." Assessment is central to the workshop, helping workshop organizers modify current strategies and plan for the future.

Implementation of the Model

The purpose of the remainder of this essay is to describe the participation of a group of teachers in workshops based on the model and to present their reactions and assessment. The method of assessment consisted of course evaluations by teachers, content analysis of teachers' writings and suggestions, and teacher interviews conducted after school was well under way in the fall. Although the interviews were intended to determine how valuable the learning from the workshops was to teachers in their own schools and classrooms, they also revealed unexpected problems that teachers may encounter when they return to their schools with a new expertise.

The thirty-six secondary teachers who participated in the in-service opportunities were veterans of the profession and came from a wide variety of schools and communities. The average length of experience was fifteen years, and no teacher had fewer than five or more than thirty-three years of experience. Six taught language arts in the junior high; the remaining thirty worked in high schools.

The size of the schools ranged from 126 students for grades nine through twelve in rural Illinois to 2,300 students in a vocational high school in Chicago.

The participants themselves were involved professionals who prided themselves on keeping abreast of developments in the teaching of English. Ten were department heads at their respective schools and had applied for the workshops, in part, to take back what they learned to other members of their departments. Several were active members of the Illinois Association of Teachers of English (IATE) and had presented papers at the annual meetings. The self-selection process of teachers for both workshops probably resulted in participants who were at once more highly motivated and more actively involved in professional development than a randomly selected sample of their colleagues.

The workshops consisted of forty-eight hours of meetings in a computer-equipped classroom. Each teacher had a computer for his or her personal use during class sessions, and computer sites on campus were available for work outside of class. For the summer workshop, participants lived together in a dormitory where they shared meals and saw one another every day. In the classroom-laboratory, teachers were taught the *Volkswriter* word-processing package on networked IBM-XT computers supported by a Hewlett-Packard laser printer. This, then, was the setting in which teachers met for class and ultimately came to share their successes, failures, and complaints of learning and writing with computers.

Each day that participants met for class, they practiced writing on word processors while responding to the various readings and to their experiences with computers. They then discussed the advantages and disadvantages of the technology from the standpoint both of learners and of teachers. To give themselves a chance to articulate their views and to gain practice composing at the word processor, they kept three online files that they added to as the workshops progressed. The first was a computer daybook, in which they recorded their reactions to learning, writing, and teaching with word processing; the second was a response file in which they wrote ten-minute reactions to their readings; the third was a summary file that served as a record of their readings as well as a source for ideas. These three online files enabled participants to assess the role of computers as composition tools and to synthesize their learning from the workshop. They then shared some of these writings with one another during class, often refining their ideas in light of others' perceptions. The aim of these procedures was to offer methods for the participants to teach writing with computers to their own students. In other words, the model requires participants to use computers and to react to readings for the course in the same way they might ask their own students to write and respond – but with different content.

Evaluation of the Model

Several instruments were used to assess the merit of the in-service approach. Some were designed especially to determine teachers' proficiency and comfort with word processing; for others, the purpose was to find out how teachers felt about the value of computers in composition instruction and, more specifically, to assess the worth of the model. The participants' computer daybooks were a particularly rich source of information regarding their experiences with computers. Typical prompts for these entries asked teachers to describe their favorite keys on the computer, to elaborate on their worst experience with word processing, or to portray the class as outsiders might see it. In describing the workshop as an outsider, one participant wrote:

> Anyone coming in would see a group of students. It doesn't matter that we are all older – I think we have that haunted student look. It is the look that says, "I feel foolish because I don't know this," or "I can't believe I just did that!" But I think our collective sense of purpose shows too. We are not here on a lark or because we don't have anything else to do. We are serious students. A few moments in conversation with a random selection of us would make that clear.

Another, in response to the same prompt, added:

> The outsider is the man in each of our English departments who hasn't been back to school since he got his bachelor's degree in 1954. He has since openly scoffed at computers for English students. When he comes to visit our classroom, he hears noise. Our fingers clicking on the keyboards, the background hum of the system, people collaborating with one another as they write. No learning here, he decides. He retreats to the security of his classroom, teacher's desk at the front, students sitting in precisioned rows.

Perhaps more than anything, the responses in the computer daybooks suggested a pride in having tackled this strange new tool and succeeded. They also point to a sense of humor, something participants never lost despite the sometimes disappearing files or ruined floppy disks. During the summer workshop another teacher wrote the following when participants were asked to explain what they didn't like about word processing:

> I really like writing with a computer, but if I have to complain, I will. I don't like the uncertainty of storing files. I've had no unhappy personal experience, but I know some people just up and lose them. I also don't like staring at those fuzzy little monitors in the dorm. Now I just kicked out the plug and lost the entire entry – so what you see is a rewrite. But I still like the computer.

The most common answer to the question of what teachers didn't like about word processing was "I can't think of anything I don't like about writing on the computer." When complaints appeared, they often were expressions of regret at not having a computer for work at home. During the interviews that took place well after the workshops, we learned that four teachers had bought computers for their work after participating in the program.

After the In-Service Experience

The responses we've reproduced so far have more to do with the participant's relationship with writing and computers than with the pedagogical uses to which the program could be applied. A more valid assessment concerned what participants did when they returned to their schools the following fall. An analysis of the content of the fall interviews revealed that many of the teachers were using computers for instruction and that some, who didn't have computer labs available, were using word processing for their own work. Still others were applying the reading and writing strategies for their classes but without computers.

More than half the participants reported that they were teaching writing with word processing. When asked what this instruction entailed, some teachers indicated that their students were participating in a writing lab once a week, to do prewriting and drafting activities on computers, and then, for the rest of the week, returning to class for peer group work in preparation for their final drafts. Other teachers said their students came every day to the lab, where classes were conducted in much the same way that the workshop had been run. Students were asked to keep online daybooks and reading journals, which they shared with one another as sources for later writings. Still other teachers noted that they hadn't had time to find out how they might use the computer lab for their English students. Two teachers reported that, although microcomputers were used in other classes in their schools, they were not available to English students.

The six teachers who had computers available for their classes and had implemented the reading and writing strategies were optimistic about the workshop's model but also cautious. For teaching literature, two of the teachers had dropped the summary writing but began each of their classes with ten-minute writings in response to short stories the students had read the night before. They both reported that this procedure seemed to ensure more thoughtful and informed discussions than they had previously expected. Another teacher said that he assigned the summaries, which he thought helped students master the subject matter, but wondered whether students were progressing beyond the summaries. That is, his students seemed unable to detect patterns among their readings or to list ideas from the reading that they could then develop more fully, as we had done in the workshop. He was continuing to experiment with his teaching strategies to find the proper balance between reading, discussion, and writing with computers during each class period. These teachers' enthusiasm for the use of computers, however, was less cautious. All were excited by the students' response to the technology and thought that the students seemed more enthusiastic about their writing when they could use word processing. Their major complaint was the insufficient computer-laboratory time available for English students in their school.

Computer training for some of the teachers also seemed to have important professional implications. Unexpectedly, when the teachers returned to work the following fall, several were greeted with new computer labs. One participant stated, "Not only was there a fully equipped computer lab for the English classes, but

I was the one saying, 'I'll figure out how to do that.' It was a big surprise to me and the rest of the department." She was not alone. Five others encountered new microcomputer labs. When we interviewed them, these teachers were busy instructing other members of their department in word processing and its applications for teaching. They were, in fact, assuming heavier workloads.

Thus there were disturbing as well as promising developments when the workshop participants returned to their schools. Several teachers felt that their political status had been advanced as a result of their workshop participation. One had been promoted to department chairperson, she thought, partially because of her new familiarity with computers. She had been given released time for her new duties as department chair, duties that included writing a curriculum to incorporate computers into composition instruction. Her new assignment meant that she was now teaching five classes instead of the customary six – still a crowded schedule of regular teaching duties, in addition to her responsibilities as chair. From another perspective, then, the change was not so much an increase in status as an added burden of work in an already full schedule.

In at least three other cases, participants were rewarded for their newfound and hard-earned expertise by being given heavier workloads. One teacher was working on Saturdays to train others in his department to teach with word processing; another, who had taken over the computer lab because no one else from the English department was interested in using it, was now also responsible for keeping the department's inventory on computers; and still another was using his planning period, wedged in between six classes, to learn a new word-processing package so that he, at his principal's request, could teach a class on computers the following semester. Teachers were not complaining – they accepted their new work with equanimity. It seems obvious, however, that these competent professionals needed more released time to help introduce technology into their English programs.

Through our interviews, we also learned of schools' scheduling problems with computers. One participant mentioned that she was now holding class in the computer lab for eight days during the semester and teaching students word processing. We assumed that the students, once trained in word processing, then visited the lab at other times, but this was not the case. The students could not practice what they had learned after the eight-day introduction, since the lab was always scheduled with classes. Other teachers noted similar scheduling problems that prevented them from using computers in ways they deemed pedagogically sound.

Participants left the course with newfound energy and knowledge but, because they were given too much work or had too little support, were sometimes unable to carry out what they had learned. These situations are distressing, since they present dilemmas that in-service training alone cannot solve. It may, however, be able to help, if the in-service experience is enlisted to mitigate the problems. That is, by using the workshops to create a network of experienced professionals, teachers can rely on one another for advice in dealing with these problems. Thus the in-service experience can become not only a foundation on which to build professional expertise but also a source of trained colleagues to whom teachers may look for mutual support and needed help.

Most teachers in the workshops formed strong attachments to one another and became a cohesive group. Participants showed their pride by designing T-shirts with a workshop logo and by compiling and publishing a set of their writings, on their own, through a local copy shop. They also kept in touch when the course ended. The sense of community emerged as a central theme in the teachers' daybooks. Asked what someone enrolling in the workshop the following year should be told, one participant wrote:

> You can look forward to an experience you won't soon forget. Warning: Be prepared to read, read, read and write, write, write. Word processing is fun. The reading of new ideas, new theories, new trends in the teaching of English challenges you to rework your own philosophy. But the most exciting part of the workshop is the peer interaction (to use a phrase we know well). Being with teachers from different backgrounds and from different parts of the state was fun. As the days turned into weeks, we stayed longer and longer at meals; spent late evenings – 10:30 on – in the lounge conferring, commiserating, communing with each other about computers, about theories, about teaching, about life. The microcosm of our class represents graduate school at its best because of the camaraderie.

It was this spirit of camaraderie that seemed to contribute most significantly to the participants' enthusiasm and confidence in using computers. Although the teachers found the curriculum useful, it was primarily their colleagues who made the workshop a memorable experience.

Some Final Comments

Computers afford an especially fruitful opportunity for working with teachers, since teachers find the machines innovative and inviting but also intimidating. The newness of the technology, moreover, generates enthusiasm and eagerness while at the same time producing fear and anxiety, all states of mind that are uncharacteristic of the in-service context. This context, at once benign and threatening (English teachers are not expected to know computers, but they are expected to know how to write), can be used to encourage veteran teachers to take risks in their own learning and teaching – to try something new. The model presented here uses this context to introduce reading and writing strategies that participants can then adapt to their own teaching with their own students.

With careful, collaborative planning with teachers in the field, in-service training in computers and composition does not have to be hampered by participants' resistance and resentment. English teachers readily learn how to use computers and, in the process, become informed critics and proponents of the new technology. Yet to have a more lasting effect on teachers themselves and thus on the schools in which they teach, in-service workshops can do more than deliver instruction. They can give teachers the opportunity to form professional relationships, which, in turn, enable them to learn from one another. By continuing to scrutinize various in-service approaches, we, as a profession, can begin to design programs in a context that overcomes teachers' resistance to both in-service training and computers.

Note

[1] The author is indebted to James Raths, Janet Eldred, Alan Purves, and Cynthia Selfe for their comments on earlier versions of this essay and to Fay Rouseff-Baker, Bernadette Easley, Catherine Thurston, Suzanne Ross, and Anna Soter for their assistance with the implementation and evaluation of the in-service model.

Assessing the Professional Role of the English Department "Computer Person"

Ellen McDaniel

◆

In his 1983 *College English* article, "Toward a Taxonomy of Scholarly Publication," I. Hashimoto proposes that the English academic profession adopt a new and more efficient classification system for describing, evaluating, and ranking scholarly activities. The system that Hashimoto proposes is "roughly built" around classifications and pictures of World War II naval vessels. By way of illustration, he offers "ten of the most significant kinds of academic publishing" ranked from one to ten, with Fleet Aircraft Carriers at the top (powerful theoretical works that shape disciplines) and Oilers at the bottom (e.g., commercial textbooks and *Cliffs Notes*). Hashimoto's article and the taxonomy it explains comprise a masterful extended satire of the profession's ongoing "responsible discussion" of scholarly publication. With his article (classified by its ship icon as a PT Boat), Hashimoto launches a vessel that is – according to the definitions of his taxonomy – an "offensive weapon that is also well suited for rescue work" (500–02).

Hashimoto's farcical taxonomy might in fact be a welcomed improvement over the ill-considered, biased, or random procedures for scholarly evaluation applied in many of our academic institutions. However, if we ignore this irony and allow satire to fulfill its rehabilitative intent, then we will know that we are to consider seriously the rescue operation that Hashimoto recommends: that is, to resist any rigid categorical and quantifying system of evaluation for scholarly activity. Such a system reduces, trivializes, and falsifies the work it tries to judge; and when its inadequacies are discovered, it is the system itself that is reduced, either suspected as invalid or scorned as ridiculous.

Hashimoto's levity is welcome in the sober and long discussions of how to evaluate the performance of academics. Certainly, we are not the only members of academia trying to feel our way toward fair practices of scholarly assessment. Our colleagues from Anthropology to Zoology debate this issue with us as they face the same realities of dropping enrollments, reduced budgets, and yet heightened demands from the public for better-equipped – not just educated – college graduates and for faculty research that can keep the country on the "cutting edge." To meet these public injunctions, academic departments have had to diversify their research and educational offerings, cross over traditional boundaries to work with other academic departments or directly with business and industry, and explore the influence and use of computer technology in their disciplines (Labin and Villella; Slaughter). No fixed system of faculty and staff evaluation can be constructed to assess these changing activities in the university, although every day, university administrators attempt to do exactly that (Deshler; DeYoung; Moses; Reisman).

The English department – like other departments – is also having to change to meet fluctuating demands; and as one of the university's most traditional departments, it is having difficulty both in admitting and in evaluating new avenues of teaching and research (Ekman). Many faculty members are still resisting the expansion of technical-writing and composition studies in their departments (Hairston; Horner; Jay Robinson). Hashimoto holds his mirror up to us so that we can see this rigidity in its most humorous light. Hazard S. Adams, however, puts the mirror under our nose and checks for signs of breath, fearing that the rigidity may in fact be departmental rigor mortis setting in. In his article "How Departments Commit Suicide," Adams offers four principles for English departments to follow in preserving not just their health but their lives. Two of the four warn against rigidity, or the "garrison mentality," whereby "strategies of department self-protection are self-defeating and can lead to suicide" ("Principle the Second," pp. 8–12), and "disciplinary purity breeds self-destruction" ("Principle the Fourth," pp. 12–13). Adams explains:

> The most common and most pernicious strategy is to resist every possibility of reaching out beyond the department's so-called traditional boundaries. It must first be remembered that on the grounds of history alone English departments are relatively new phenomena and need not regard what they should or should not do as chiseled in stone. To build one's program and faculty entirely around the protection of the major is almost certainly to limit future possibilities, which are so often generated by fortunate chance or unexpected opportunities. Such closing in is found also in time to be erosive of student interest and respect. (8)

My purpose in providing this background is to remind us of what nontraditional faculty members confront when they try to pursue their research and teaching interests with the hope of gaining some support or reward for it – tenure, promotion, raises, and other forms of advancement – from tradition-minded English or humanities departments (Ekman). I follow this caution with a case study of a particular non-traditional department member now resident in most English and humanities departments – the so-called computer person – whose career health I try to assess in light of the two articles about the profession that I have just discussed. The situation of this faculty member will no doubt be of interest and use to the primary readers of this collection, who are in all likelihood "computer persons" themselves, and who at some point will have to describe and defend their work in their home departments (Holdstein, "Politics"). However, I hope also to reach a larger audience of English professionals by joining the "responsible discussion" (no irony this time) of the scholarly activity in our changing departments. With this article, I introduce these "computer people" in our departments and try both to describe and to explain their application of computer technology to the study and teaching of English. I argue for the support of these people, whose appearance is recent, whose teaching is nontraditional, and whose research is often unfamiliar and perplexing. They are among those who can be victimized by the established categories and measures of evaluation in traditional English and humanities departments, but who, I believe, have appeared at one of those "moments of intellectual opportunity" that Adams advises us to seize, nurture, and bring to life in order to invigorate the larger body English that must survive for the sake of all of us.

Profile: Who the Computer Person Is and Is Not

Because so many of our colleagues in all areas of English studies employ the computer as a word processor, the principal computer user in our departments is that person who uses the computer extensively as a tool in teaching and research – in whatever field she or he is in – or who has made the computer the subject of teaching or research, such as in the study of the computer's influence on writing or literature. Typically, these persons engaged in computer-based research and teaching (1) use the advanced features of word processing (formatting macros or stylesheets and document retrieval); (2) use software other than word processing in their teaching and research (computer-assisted-instruction programs, software for stylistic and statistical analysis, graphics, desktop publishing); or (3) fulfill the department "service" obligation by taking responsibility for computer acquisition and use in the department (e.g., sitting on computer committees, writing specifications for department computers, instructing colleagues in their use, introducing business computing to the administrative staff). The "computer people" are perceived as being nontraditional in their teaching, research, and service interests, though, in time, their interests may become the common domain of all English scholars, just as word processing has. Because it is likely that their novel use of the computer may not remain novel for long, it is important not to confuse the tools or instruments of research with the research or the researchers themselves (likewise with teaching). Tools must be understood and evaluated, just as theories and methods are, but they are not the only, or always the most important, feature about the work done or the person doing the work.

Thus I use the term *computer person* somewhat ironically. The term has stuck to these people who use the computer as a tool, though in fact, they are specialists in English studies first, not in computers. The novelty of using a computer in English studies seems, at first glance, to be the most important characteristic of these people (Baron). However, their degrees are exactly like those of their colleagues in Renaissance literature, modern literature, or rhetoric and composition. They wince at being called a computer "wizard" or "guru," for most are neither programmers nor hardware technicians. They often are as mystified as the novice by much of the machine's workings and operations. Though suspected by some to be the fallen angels of the humanities – descended into the pit of unholy technocracy, the conservative right, and talking Coke machines – they are not. In fact, their appreciation of the power, intelligence, imagination, and sensibility that can never reside in a computer program may be as great as or greater than that of their most computer-suspicious colleagues. Frequently, they are the computer's greatest skeptics and critics (Jobst, "Word Processing"; Schwartz, "Monsters"; Selfe and Hawisher; Selfe and Wahlstrom, "Benevolent Beast").

Since 1983, the *MLA Job Information List* has shown a marked increase in advertisements for people with computer training or experience, mostly for those who can bring that experience to technical writing and rhetoric and composition programs. Previously, most of the people eligible to apply for such positions would have acquired their experience after receiving their degrees, and so would be coming from postgraduate positions or jobs. Today, graduate programs in rhetoric, composition, and technical writing around the country are beginning to produce writing specialists with heightened computer awareness and appreciation and more and more experience in applying computers in teaching and research. The rhetoric and composition programs, with their extensive interdisciplinary overlap with other fields, have been brought into contact with computers through (1) the word processor, which most writing specialists acknowledge is a revolutionary writing technology with possible revolutionary effects on language and communication, and (2) linguistic, psychological, and educational research, which is largely empirical and thus computer-driven. As a result, more of the new rhetoric, composition, and technical writing positions that require people with computer expertise will be filled with new graduates. Texas A&M University was one of the first to acquire such a specialist straight out of graduate school when it hired Paul Meyer, a 1985 graduate of the University of Texas English department. Meyer's research at UT in the rhetoric and composition program was done under Stephen Witte and was largely empirical, interdisciplinary, and computer-intensive.

Still – albeit less frequently – the person most engaged in computer-based research and teaching in the English department may be a member of the literature faculty, introduced to the computer by bibliographic work, concordance making, or article writing. Such a person discovers and becomes enthusiastic about the tools available to aid academic research, from automatic spellers and indexing programs to software for document retrieval and desktop publishing. Robert C. Leitz, at Louisiana State University, Shreveport, for example, has made extensive use of computers in his work on the Jack London papers. Others find themselves coerced into learning something about computers and end up writing books about them. Alan T. McKenzie, at Purdue University, had his eighteenth-century head turned by computers when his administrative work as assistant department chair required that he purchase the department's first word-processing equipment. He went on to write one of the first books about computers in the profession, *A Grin on the Interface*. Occasionally, the resident computer expert is a full professor in the established center of English department studies. I think especially of Harrison T. Meserole processing thousands of records through his IBM PC-AT for the *International Shakespeare Bibliography*; his lecture "Shakespeare in the Second Age of Science" is a fascinating study and tribute to what the computer has been able to do to make centuries of Shakespearian study available and usable.

However, few English departments are specifically hiring computer-and-literature people, except perhaps for bibliographers. The computer's greater usefulness as a tool for writing than for reading accounts for its predominance in the writing fields. Ironically, it was as a reading tool that many writing faculty members first explored the computer – and for a very practical reason. During the brief period when computers were the exclusive property of faculty members, many hoped that the computer would be a paper grader and thus relieve them of a burden that can often take the fun out of writing classes. The computer has proved to be of only minimal use as a grading tool, but its strength as a writing tool was quickly discovered and pursued vigorously. A survey of the programs for the College Composition and Communication Conference since 1983 will show this shift of emphasis and also reveal how rapidly the number of writing-and-computing specialists has grown. The CCCC programs and those of NCTE taken together provide a representative and informative list of these specialists and the work in which they are engaged.

In general, as Deborah Holdstein has observed, the computer people in English departments are typically as young as the technology they use. They are the new rhetoric, composition, and technical-writing specialists, recently graduated, untenured, and with the double onus of being suspect as much for their writing degree as for their computer expertise. (English departments are still trying to work out the connections between literature and writing, and the specter of technology knocking at the door not long after the rhetoric and composition program gained entry has shaken some traditional English faculty.) Most of these people in computers and writing have had to learn what they know about computers on their own. It is not possible to coast long on even last year's computer course; the technology turns over too rapidly. As a rule, they discovered computers in serendipitous or free-lance ways, by association with computer-obsessed family members or friends, through jobs that brought them in contact with the machines, or simply out of curiosity. Thus the people working with computers are seldom able to produce a long transcript of computer courses taken, and rarely do they have a degree for this collateral field they have chosen. They have worked independently to master this discipline – one that requires skills, techniques, and thinking quite different from those required in traditional English studies – and to keep up with it, they read the current books and journals in the field, as all active academics do. In addition, however, and just as important, is the knowledge they acquire through the manuals and trade literature, the manufacturers' catalogs of hardware and software, the telephone hotlines, the computer teleconferences, and, of course, the computer itself, by working on it day in and day out.

Computer technology has penetrated into all corners of the university. By now, most departments have discovered that there is a technological dimension to their discipline. Because individuals of like interests will gravitate to each other, academics using computer technology are reaching across departmental boundaries to find each other (Baron). Just as teachers of American literature band together because their common interests have made them friends or their similar professional and political concerns have made them allies, people with computer expertise find colleagues, friends, and allies in other departments or agencies of the university. Because they come from many places in the university, they officially collect themselves in faculty users groups, various university and college computer committees, and on administrative staffs of computer facilities. By many accounts their influence often flourishes there, although it must struggle hard to survive in the home department (Labin and Villella).

Nevertheless, I would not argue for resolving this struggle by moving all computer-based study and teaching to the computer science department, just as I would not argue for moving all language-based study and teaching into the English department. The departments of English and computer science have in common their connection to all other disciplines, the former through language and its expression and the latter through computer technology. There is no field that these two departments do not touch with their tools. However, a tool needed for problem solving should reside where the problems are solved; it is neither practical nor desirable to move the problems to the tool. Thus, in the case of computers, the machines should exist on site in the departments that need them and not be confined and isolated in a center of service or utility. By the same token, the people working with computers in English studies – although they stand on the boundaries of two departments – should remain in the home department and bring to it the technical tools that are available for performing language study and solving language problems.

Production: The Fruit of Labor and Its Value

Fortunately, journals are available for the publication of work in computers and English studies. The journals range from widely circulated but well-respected magazines, such as *Byte*, to our profession's own *College Composition and Communication* and *College English*. In fact, many of these journals have solicited articles on computer applications in language, communication, and literary study. Likewise, book publishers have thrust the computer into high visibility, and the MLA and NCTE have joined this effort with their own publications. The professional conferences also hold numerous computer sessions, with one or more at every scheduled time period of the CCCC and NCTE conferences since 1983. The linguistics societies have been discussing computers for a long time, and the list of computer sessions grows yearly at the MLA convention. There is tacit if not tangible approval by our societies, our journal editors, and our book publishers that computer technology is worthy of merging with our traditional studies and merits space in print. Although most of our mainstream publications have been willing to publish this research, there remains much work that does not fit within the scope of our traditional journals. For that reason, the work of computer-and-writing researchers may appear in nontraditional places, such as the publications of other disciplines and societies (e.g., the journals of the Institute of Electrical and Electronics Engineers or the Association of Computing Machinery), in such "glossies" as *PC Magazine* or *Educational Technology*, or in the few truly interdisciplinary journals that exist, such as *Computers and the Humanities* and *Computers and Composition*.

Unfortunately, these journals are usually unknown to English faculty members, and what is unknown is often judged as inferior. The prestigious journal names have become locked in, and the acknowledgment of a new contender comes slowly, if at all. If the journal means little to a teacher, the article published in it often means less. Thus the double ignorance about the research itself and the publication vehicle that transports it leaves such researchers vulnerable to misinterpretation and prejudice. Certainly, researchers in language and computers are not the first to complain that their work is unappreciated, misunderstood, and, as a result, wrongly evaluated by their colleagues. However, this common grievance among academics standing for promotion or tenure, or waiting for a job offer, particularly holds true for the new teachers and researchers in computers and English studies. Not only is their field new, employing unfamiliar tools, methods, approaches, and theories, but it is a discipline about which many people readily admit their ignorance. In the evaluation process, these computer people frequently confront colleagues who, although loath to admit an unfamiliarity with any subject in the field of English, will freely and even boastfully confess their lack of computer knowledge (see, for example, Ohmann).

Not knowing about computers is a legitimate and forgivable ignorance. To be antitechnology is both approved and sanctioned in English and humanities departments, although not likely to be so always. Surprisingly, however, an academic with computer expertise may find the computer "illiteracy" of colleagues both an advantage and a disadvantage. It is a disadvantage, of course, for the reasons I have just mentioned and for smaller annoyances – for instance, when one has to repair the problems that arise when colleagues do not read manuals, fail to back up diskettes, or leave half their lunches on (read "in") the keyboard. The computer person often spends too much time on technical maintenance, usually because departments and universities still do not put adequate money aside to maintain the machinery after they purchase it. In addition, because computers are costly to run, maintain, upgrade, and replace, they compete for department resources and are unpopular among department members who believe that the machines should not be there in the first place. Computer people often find themselves in the uncomfortable position of lobbying for resources that computer-suspicious faculty want to spend in other ways. It is safer to stay in the library where the competition for books is less severe or at least anonymous. What is more, the computer person has the unenviable task of taking care of everything that has to do with computers in the department, from writing technical specifications on purchase orders and keeping inventory, to responding to surveys about educational technology that the department head receives. Such activities can easily fulfill the individual's faculty service obligation, but how that contribution is perceived varies from department to department. Some departments value the work; many do not.

Finally, in addition to employing computers in research activities and department service, the computer person generally will take on the task of introducing them in the classroom or writing lab. This is an enormous job, complicated by many logistical, administrative, political, financial, and pedagogical issues. Getting students to the computers, or the computers to them, involves a litany of responsibilities and concerns: justification, access, scheduling, monitoring, assistance, security, repair, maintenance, and so on. Also, instructional materials have to be changed, reshaped, or created anew to accompany the technology. Such effort is necessary and important and should be credited as such, but often it goes unnoticed.

Paradoxically, the advantages in being the computer person often spring from the same factors that make it a disadvantage. Although English and humanities departments do not clearly understand computer-based research, it does not seem to reap the disdain that other new research pursuits have had to suffer, such as rhetoric and composition research, which in large part paved the way for the computer's entrance into the discipline. The computer is so much an unknown to many of our colleagues that it has become something of a mystery. The whole world is grappling with technological issues, so no one, not even the most dyed-in-the-wool medievalist, can say that the concerns are inconsequential. In fact, there is something medieval in the awe that even the most distrustful have for people who use computers competently, something akin to the respect shown in the fourteenth century for a sorcerer or a wizard. No one ever dismisses computer competency as useless or soft, although some people may find research in the teaching applications of computers an inappropriate or even sinister pursuit for the English department to engage in. Ironically, a department member who is retrieving a lost file for a colleague, or assembling a computer system for the writing lab, or bringing up the library's card catalog on the department computer, may be earning his or her colleagues' most genuine and profound admiration (but whether as a technician or an academic, I cannot say).

Other advantages lie in the alliances computer researchers make outside the department and the knowledge they acquire there. First of all, possibilities open up for secure and stimulating employment in other fields and professions, both within and outside the university. As a result, a computer specialist loses some of the professional vulnerability he or she had as an Arnoldian or a Conradian. Second, other kinds of support are available for the researcher's work. Financial assistance and equipment are often provided by companies, foundations, and business associations to help ease the difficulties in getting resources from the department or the university. Third, and most important, the researcher's acquaintance with new minds and methods creates possibilities for research collaboration and interdisciplinary study. New vehicles for performing and disseminating research include networked computer systems, which make databases, electronic mail, and teleconferences available to use and learn from on a daily and hourly basis, not just monthly, quarterly, or annually, as with our research literature (see Spitzer, in this volume); software design and development offer additional channels for research dissemination. Many of the computer people in English departments have turned their energies to writing software, especially for computer-assisted instruction, editing, style analysis, natural-language processing, and translation.

The problem remains, however, that the department may not value these new skills, products, contacts, resources, and recognition. To be sure, such nontraditional research products as computer software are hard to review. They cannot be taken home to read in bed. A system has to be assembled of coordinated and compatible hardware and software. The system must then be accessible to user-reviewers, who also need the operational skill and/or assistance to run it. More important, the reviewers must understand what they are looking at and looking for. The sophistication or significance of a software product will not be discernible to an untrained reviewer. To describe what goes into software design and development would go beyond the scope of this paper. However, to summarize, the quality of software is determined by (1) the adequacy or excellence of the theory underpinning the design, (2) the effectiveness of the graphics and screen displays, (3) the programming skill and use of appropriate language(s) and techniques, (4) the appropriateness of the computer as a vehicle for the subject matter, and (5) the successful integration of these and other elements. (Note that in the Hashimoto taxonomy, CAI programs are classified as "Oilers," highly important but low-prestige vessels akin to television productions.)

The skepticism (or distrustfulness) of the department stems from a source deeper than just the difficulty in evaluating software. The design and development of software is work that most frequently brings computer experts on the faculty into association with the computer industry and its commercial extensions. Collaboration with business and industry in performing academic research is perhaps the most unusual and perplexing feature about such faculty members that English and humanities departments have to evaluate. Contract money and obligations are not clearly understood or trusted in colleges of humanities, as they are in colleges of engineering, agriculture, and business. Confusion abounds in a faculty when one of its members teaches fewer classes than everyone else; has an office full of computer equipment; has special funds for supplies, travel, and staff; and publishes technical reports, manuals, and software rather than *PMLA* articles or Twayne books. Traditionally, English departments have suspected collaboration because they cannot know exactly what the contribution of each participant has been, and, more to the point, they maintain the unshakable view that the best scholarship is a solitary, inexpensive, and reclusive activity. However, collaboration with business and industry, or with other academics in the university, is both common and necessary for interdisciplinary and computer-based research. An appreciation of the need for such collaboration is lacking in English and humanities departments, which ought to become more open to the notion of research partnerships.

No doubt, the teachers and researchers in the field of computers and English studies will continue to be judged by the same criteria that inspired Hashimoto's taxonomy. They will need to publish more Battleships, Cruisers, and Destroyers and fewer Cargo Ships, Oilers, and Salvage Vessels. Thus we can be grateful that the "best" journals show themselves willing to publish such research. Also, new journals in the field, such as *Computers and Composition* and *Research in Word Processing Newsletter*, are gathering prestige as journals of specialization. However, it is likely that some of the specialty journals will disappear as the traditional and established journals publish more and more of the research. Computers will be brought into the mainstream of research in English studies and eventually will hold little novelty but more respect as an established research tool and subject for study. The scholars pursuing this research will find themselves less anomalous and alone. Already, the "computer person" is metamorphosing into a "computer community."

In the meantime, more informed and sympathetic evaluation of the work and products of teachers and researchers in this field is needed. To facilitate this goal, some of the interdisciplinary journals that I have mentioned might be subscribed to and brought into the home department library so that more faculty members can see and read them. To introduce colleagues both to the journals and to the research, issues with articles that have to do with computer applications in English studies might be circulated among faculty members. Of course, more computers inside the department itself will do much to acquaint colleagues with computer-based research and teaching. To support the use of hardware, short courses in special word-processing features, information retrieval, hypertext programs, desktop publishing, and so forth, might be organized and offered to faculty members. It would also be wise for English departments to find out more about sponsored research other than grants and fellowships by exploring how departments that regularly handle such research contracts evaluate and approve them.

The academic world changes; so does its scholarly activity, including the tools, methods, and means used to perform it. Categorical and quantifying systems for evaluating research fail to capture what is important about it. Ironically, the tool that administrators use to put such evaluation criteria and procedures in place is the computer, and we see here one of its limitations. It does not assess and judge people well, not even so-called computer people. These researchers are newcomers to the game, especially in the humanities, and their work must be judged for the good it does and not by how it conforms or does not conform to the established notions of what research is. Evaluation that is tolerant of difference, open-minded in application, and an encouragement to experimentation and change should remain the order of the day in the university.

Computers in English Departments: The Rhetoric of Techno/Power

Cynthia L. Selfe

———◆———

People who say that the last battles of the computer revolution in English departments have been fought and won don't know what they're talking about. If our current use of computers in English studies is marked by any common theme at all, it is experimentation at the most basic level. As a profession, we are just learning how to live with computers, just beginning to integrate these machines effectively into writing- and reading-intensive courses, just starting to consider the implications of the multilayered literacy associated with computers. In our departments, we have only begun to see possibilities for using computers to encourage collaboration and communication among colleagues, to ease secretarial burdens, to support research and publication projects, to make scholarship accessible.

If we have learned anything about computers, it is that they can have a dramatic (some, here, would argue "drastic") effect on the social systems we call English departments. Like other communities in which people are bound by close ties of language, commitment, shared interests, or living arrangements, English departments are composed of intimately networked components: people, facilities, curricula, computers are only a few. Each of these components, we know from personal experience, is dependent on others; each influences others in a dynamic dance of social and political interaction.

And yet, when I get the opportunity to help faculty members and chairs integrate computers into their departments, seldom will these colleagues speculate with me about the social impact the new technology might have. Most of them want to talk about computers: about hardware and software, networks and configurations, monitors and memory, cost and space. Few colleagues are willing to plan for the people who use the machines: to think about how computers can and will affect departmental communications, change academic roles, alter productivity, modify traditional lines of power and interaction, or encourage different attitudes toward scholarly involvement.

And herein lies the topic of this paper.[1] As a profession, we have learned that integrating computers into English departments will have an immediate and significant impact on the social systems and the communications that occur within our academic communities. In English departments, then, we would be well advised to plan deliberately and systematically for these changes, identifying strategic, contextual frameworks for computer integration that will tie technological decisions directly to the academic life and work of the department. Such plans should ensure that the introduction of computers is not driven by hardware choices, software preferences, seniority, or any other single aspect of departmental concern, but by programmatic efforts that grow out of the communal understanding and direction of a given faculty.

If we are visionary enough in our strategic plans for computer integration, both within our departments and within our profession, we can use the new technology to create changes in English departments that we have been wanting to see for some time now; we can use computers to support, in an electronic sense, Arthur Young's notion of English departments as social collectives, intellectual discourse communities that revolve around a common set of goals.[2]

If we are not so visionary, if we do not answer some of the more difficult questions about computers, our use of these machines will precipitate petrifaction of the existing system rather than change. In this case, computers can support those characteristics of English departments of which we are not so proud: the unproductive competition, the political hegemony, the abuse of part-timers and secretaries, and the segmentation of information and communication.

The Implications of Techno/Power

I can begin my support of these statements by identifying a second important piece of information our profession has discovered about computers: there is great power associated with their use. Academics who are new to computers and see only the positive aspects of this phenomenon generally refer to the issue as one of "empowerment"– implying that if individuals can learn to use computers, to master the intricacies of a particular word-processing package or a spreadsheet program, they will have gained important and valuable access to information.

Indeed, many departments use this line of reasoning to sell their faculty and staff members on training programs in computer literacy. Faculty members are told, for instance, that if they learn to use a computer, they can tap into national conferences on Bitnet or Telenet, do online searches of libraries, and correspond daily with colleagues from other universities. Secretaries are told that they can revise documents with ease, store records in less space, routinize personnel and budget reports. All this is true, of course.

But there are other, and darker, sides to this issue as well. Techno/power – to use Colette Dowling's term[3] – involves financial and personal costs. In most departments, computers must be purchased piecemeal, one or two at a time, and often at the expense of other educational resources our profession values – books, travel, release time. Techno/power has a social cost as well. In a community, when one group is empowered, another may see itself as lacking power, especially when technology is involved. As early as 1980, Dowling was writing about the developing war between the "techno/crats" and the "techno/peasants":

> Technocrats speak to one another in a new language. They talk of chunking, of networking, of gigahertz. Like the philosophers of an earlier age, they are in the position of having to create new concepts to deal with radically different ways of perceiving things foisted on them by the new information to which they're privy . . . . [They are] planning our lives. . . . accessing the hardware that will create your future . . . challenging our very definition of intelligence. (1)

In English departments, computer technology also represents a form of power, and in this power there is, as Joseph Weizenbaum points out, the potential for great good and great evil. Nowhere is the potential more apparent than in the choices English faculties will be making in the early 1990s about how to integrate computer systems and individual computers into their academic lives. These decisions will determine whether departments use computers to foster communication or to limit access to information, to bring department members together or to isolate them, to inspire a recognition of the commonweal or to support destructive competition.

Identifying Techno/Power in English Departments

To help faculty members and chairs judge for themselves how their department is faring in the allocation and use of techno/power, we can sketch some general guidelines for identifying and describing the distribution of such power in an academic community. Several issues are central in such a discussion, but we can begin with three questions about the issue of computer access:

> Who has a computer in the department?
> Where are computers located?
> What are the priorities of computer use for individuals?[4]

The most useful answers to these questions about access to techno/power require a close look at the realities of the department. Although the first question, for example, can be answered by compiling a list of individuals who have machines sitting on their desks or in their offices, we must also ask, "Why *these* individuals?" When a department purchases computers for faculty members, access is frequently, if unconsciously, tied to traditional hierarchies of rank, or to implicit or explicit departmental agendas for scholarship and research. As Edward Westcott would put it, "them that has gits."

Similarly, in asking, "Where are computers located?" faculty members must look beyond a simple answer involving location to determine who in the department has access to computers in their offices and who must use machines in public workspaces. Moreover, examining the assigned hours of access for the workspaces reveals who is limited to using a computer only during regular business hours and thus may be subject to distracting interruptions, and who can use the machines after hours, when the halls are quiet and the real work of a department gets done.

For those individuals who do not have computers in their offices, priority of access becomes important. When the number of machines or printers is limited, the method of determining who has access and when, like the method of allocating machines, directly reflects the value systems of a department. To gain insight into those values, faculty members can explore how computer time is apportioned and who in a department has responsibility for the decisions.

And yet immediate access to computers is only one kind of power associated with the new technology. Another, and perhaps more important, kind of power arises from access to *information*. Thus, in talking about power and computers, faculty members will have to describe the systems or networks to which specific computers are connected, asking questions such as the following:

> To what systems/networks are individuals' computers tied?
> How is membership to these systems/networks determined?
> On these systems/networks, to what information do individual computer users have access?
> How do individuals use information accessed through computer systems/networks?
> What is the purpose of the computer systems/networks to which individuals have access?

In answering each of these questions, faculty members might make additional notations. They can identify, for instance, whether individual colleagues have access to departmentwide, universitywide, or international networks, and how the cost of membership in connection with the networks is determined. When specific networks are considered, colleagues can learn something about the distribution of techno/power by finding out who in a department or a university controls access to information on networks and what criteria are used in controlling the access.

The last two questions in this series can help faculty members fine-tune their perception of techno/power. As teachers, we know that having access to information is of little use unless we can employ that information in a productive way. Many higher-level administrators, for example, have access to information about low salaries in our profession, but whether they use the figures in a useful way is a debatable point, indeed. Similarly, in defining techno/power, we should determine how individuals are permitted to use information they access by computer networks: whether, for example, they can use this knowledge for their own work or scholarship, as faculty members might; for the commonweal of the department, as an administrator might; or only to complete other people's work, as a secretary might. Looking at the purposes for which individuals are allowed to use computer networks helps define the distribution of techno/power in a department. For some individuals, access to networks provides an opportunity to engage in open dialogues with peers or pursue academic exchanges with colleagues, others can use networks only to receive information that has been selected for them. Power involves control of information as well as access to information. The more freedom of choice users on a network have, the more power they have.

Finally, in identifying techno/power, faculty members can look at issues of training and education. Knowledge is power, as we often tell our students, and with technology this equation remains stable. When we ask, therefore, "To what kind of training do individuals have access?" we need to determine who controls access to training in a department and what kind of training is available.

Planning for Techno/Power in English Departments

Because computers carry with them the potential for such power, departments should construct strategic plans for integrating computers that are based on contextual visions of departmental academic efforts within institutional settings. Without strategic plans of this kind, English faculties run the risk of making computer decisions on the basis of individual aspects of departmental operations and of allowing specific criteria to have undue, and thus potentially disruptive, influence. With strategic plans, English departments can monitor the impact of technology on an ongoing basis. The following suggestions provide the basis for such work.

Suggestion 1: Make computers an issue for departmental discussion and decision making. The departmental computer specialist or the chair should not have sole responsibility for the decisions made about computers; instead, as many department members as possible ought to become involved. Such a strategy will help eliminate a single-minded perspective on the complex issues surrounding computers and their use.

Noncomputer users, for instance, can give excellent suggestions about how to set up training courses that would appeal to them directly, how to locate computers so that they will receive maximum use by all members of the department, and how to distribute techno/power most equitably. Staff members – secretaries, aides, computer-lab consultants – should be involved in all discussions of hardware and software choices; they will be dealing most consistently with the equipment purchased for the department. Faculty members who already own computers can provide expertise in systems choice; in the linking of various brands of computers with electronic communications and compatibility software; and in the thorny ethical issues of software licensing, the safeguarding of privacy, and the protection of users' health and safety.

Making computers the business of the department will also inform the community about the true cost of electronic decisions. In discussions of budget allocations for computers, for instance, faculty members can learn that techno/power is frequently purchased at the cost of other resources: books, travel, personnel. In these communal discussions, faculty members can set realistic parameters on computer spending: how much the department is willing to spend on purchasing computers and updating software each year, how much on training faculty and staff members to use particular computer applications, and how much on providing its members with access to national and international computer networks.

Suggestion 2: Make computer decisions grow out of departmental goals and objectives. Decisions about computers do not have to be made in a theoretical and philosophical vacuum; existing departmental goals and objectives should inform decisions about computers and techno/power. As a community, colleagues can formulate a vision of how computers can support the mission of the department; ongoing computer decisions, like all other departmental choices, will be made on the basis of consensual agreement about these priorities.

For example, a department may recognize as five-year priorities the related goals of building a graduate program and strengthening research in rhetoric. These goals, in turn, should shape the purchase of computers and the distribution of techno/power. If the department can afford to purchase only one or two computers a year, for instance, hardware might be best allocated to those faculty or staff members working most directly on the graduate-program committee or those engaged in active scholarship in rhetoric studies. Software purchases might also be made in support of the departmental goals. For the graduate-program effort, for example, the department might purchase a scheduling program for the director of graduate studies, or membership on a network that supports interlibrary loans. For the rhetoric scholarship currently being done, the department might purchase word-processing software that facilitates indexing, footnoting, and bibliographic work; databases that can store and sort research notes and quoted material; or translation programs.

The strategy of letting departmental goals form the basis of decisions about computers also ensures that a program of technology integration is tailored specifically to the needs of a given community of scholars. Another department, which has as a primary goal increased communication among members and other scholarly communities, might make hardware and software decisions quite different from those in the previous example. Such a department might choose a networked system that would allow faculty to have online conversations or send electronic mail, modems to connect faculty with colleagues from other departments, or hard-disk storage capacity that would accommodate departmental archives of public reports and memoranda for future reference.

Suggestion 3: Keep a humanistic focus on technology. Technology and the lure of techno/power can encourage a machine-centered mentality. Departments that succumb to this view of the universe purchase computers for the features the machines have – RAM, ROM, high-resolution monitors, 20-megabyte hard disks – not for the people who will use them.

In making departmental or committee decisions about hardware and software, faculty members should think about the human beings behind the machines. Realizing that secretaries must print or complete computer-supported work for a number of faculty, for instance, may convince a departmental committee that it should adopt a standard word-processing package for everyone's use or to set aside a block of uninterrupted training time for staff members whenever a new software or hardware purchase is made. Similarly, considering the various scholarly requirements of individual faculty members may persuade a department to invest in a library of software packages that will suit individual needs and to hire a part-time consultant to train individual faculty members in the use of the software. Finally, considering the human beings who must use the machines will remind most departments of the necessity for allocating money for ergonomically sound furniture for all computer users, for public workstations available on an after-hours basis for all members of the department, and for ongoing training for both faculty and staff.

Suggestion 4: Use computers to promote community. Techno/power can be divisive. Lacking a humane, well-thought-out plan for integrating computers into the life of an academic community, departments often fall back on a nonplan of allocating computers according to the traditional academic hierarchy – the first computers go to the dean and the department head, the next batch to full professors, and so on – thus exacerbating the rigidity and the hegemony of the traditional system with the added power of technology.

In similarly well-intentioned, but less-than-effective, efforts, departments purchase individual microcomputers, place them on every faculty member's desk, and fail to exploit the potential of networked communication among users and communal discussions of departmental computer policies. Such an approach, while distributing techno/power among faculty members in a department, only encourages isolation of members of the academic community and segmentation of information within the department.

But the picture need not look so bleak. If a department uses computers to support the notion of community, it can invest in an electronic network on which colleagues can share drafts of conference papers or journal articles. Such a network can also be used to encourage the participation of marginal members of the community. Departments can set up electronic conferences on matters of governance, curriculum changes, or the use of part-time personnel; electronic polling places, in which individuals can register their votes or comments on departmental direction; and electronic archives.

The concept of building electronic community might also influence the way in which departments deal with nonstandard equipment. Departments that place a high value on communication among members within the community might publish compatibility guidelines for computers or software purchases by individual faculty members, allocate money to link existing machines to newly purchased departmental equipment, and work closely with university administrators to make sure that gifts or grants of equipment provided by specific vendors are compatible with departmental systems.

Continuing Concerns about Techno/Power

The four suggestions we have just outlined, of course, will not eliminate a department's difficulties in connection with techno/power; in fact, they may simply open the door to increasingly complicated issues. The concept, for instance, of linking departmental members by an electronic network raises as many problems as it solves. On such networks, for example, preserving individuals' rights to privacy must be a top priority (see Schwartz, in this volume). Individual department members must have the ability to protect personal documents, to tag some documents for certain readers, to lock their schedules so that they cannot be changed by others. With such a publicly inclusive system, the private files a department head must keep or the private writing a faculty member wishes to guard may be best located in a filing cabinet rather than on the computer.

Another concern departments will have in trying to implement the suggestions hinges on money. Capital investment in computers is still relatively high, as are maintenance costs, but these costs are pretty much the same for a well-planned program of computer integration and a poorly planned program; however, a well-planned program will, in the long run, be less expensive than a poorly planned program. Careful planning will eliminate many hardware/compatibility problems, wasted software dollars, and training costs. The cost of any system can be considered only in relation to its benefits.

In fact, the value of any suggestions we can make about the distribution and use of techno/power lies in a department's willingness to engage in frank and democratic exploration of communal values. If a department followed the suggestions we have provided for integrating techno/power, computers would be used to support the work that the department, as a community of individuals, values most. In this way, the purpose of the technology would be to distribute power beyond traditional hierarchical structures; to create collaborative opportunities; to invite involvement, professional development, communication. A community committed to such goals has no price.

And it is for this reason that English professionals have to begin controlling techno/power and applying it for a greater good. Unless we make decisions about computers, decisions that are shaped by our humanist training and informed by the values we would like to see at the center of English departments, these choices will be made for us. Computers, by themselves, do not create a dualistic society of "techno/crats" and "techno/peasants"—it's the people behind the machines, those who imagine the systems and run them, who wreak this kind of divisive havoc. In the same way, it's the people behind the machines who can use computers constructively to support, again in Arthur Young's terms, "rebuilding community" in English departments.

Notes

[1] This article, with the exception of minor changes, was first printed in the *ADE Bulletin* 90 (Fall 1988): 63–67.

[2] When Arthur Young's article first appeared, in the *ADE Bulletin* (Spring 1984), composition faculties were calling for secession from English departments controlled by literature faculties. His article endorsed "rebuilding community" in English departments, dissolving "the tensions between writing and literature conceptually and emotionally" by making the "study of all discourse" a common goal of these scholarly communities (24).

[3] I thank Colette Dowling, author of *The Techno/Peasant Survival Manual*, for her discussion of techno/power as that advantage of influence that grows from the control and understanding of computer technology.

[4] I designed these questions to look at techno/power in connection with department-purchased and department-owned computers. They would have to be modified for situations in which faculty members purchase their own computers for use in university offices. I have purposely limited my discussion to techno/power and its relation to faculty and staff members and administrators, leaving aside for the moment the important issues surrounding students and computers.

Who Profits from Courseware?

Lisa Gerrard

—◆—

Not long ago, few instructors thought of the commercial possibilities of instructional software – at least not at the outset. Almost all the writing instructors I spoke to became interested in designing writing software to provide a new tool for their students. Intrigued by the possibilities of computer-based composition, they learned enough *Basic* or *Pascal* to serve their needs, or they hired a programmer – almost always an undergraduate and often one of their students – and set to work. However experimental, the project was just an extension of the work they did all the time – updating and redesigning their courses.

But as the market for educational software has grown, so has its potential to generate income. Some language arts courseware has proved commercially successful. A University of Delaware package called *Latin Skills* has brought its authors thousands of dollars in royalties (Turner 24). A large package, like *HBJ Writer*, developed by the University of California, Los Angeles, has the potential to generate considerable returns for the university, the authors, and the publisher. Although educational software is unlikely to prove as lucrative as commercial packages like *Wordperfect* and *Microsoft Word*, the prospect of earning returns has interested authors and their universities in marketing their courseware. It has also raised some difficult questions: Who owns the software and who is entitled to royalties?[1]

Current Ownership Policies

Not all universities have software ownership policies, and those that do have them must decide how they will apply them to widely different projects. Traditionally, universities have treated copyrightable material – faculty members' books and articles – as the authors' property and have regarded patentable inventions as the university's property. In most cases, faculty are entitled to whatever returns their writing produces, while the university is entitled to income produced by inventions. Although a 1980 federal law stipulates that software is to be protected by copyright rather than patent, universities still have to determine who owns the copyright. The State University of New York, Stony Brook, treats software as literature and leaves the copyright to the professor (Van Arsdale 152). Other universities, however, distinguish between software and other copyrightable materials, and have a separate software policy. Some policies, like Stanford's, try to accommodate both the institution's and the author's interests by declaring software a hybrid that combines features of invention and writing (Bunting 4). As written code, software resembles a book; as a technological device operating through a machine, it resembles an invention.[2] In such cases, the university retains ownership but shares returns with the developers. As we might expect, other schools have devised variations on these policies.

Most policies focus not on the product's status as writing or invention but on the circumstances of its development. A major consideration is whether the developer uses university facilities. Faculty members who develop software at home, without university resources, usually retain ownership, although some universities claim ownership regardless of where their faculty work or whether they use institutional resources. Others, like Carnegie Mellon University, require compensation only when the use is defined as "substantial"– that is, "extensive unreimbursed use of major laboratory, studio, or computational facilities, or human resources" valued at over $5,000. This definition exempts resources such as libraries and faculty offices, which are commonly available to faculty and staff (3).

The way a project is funded affects ownership. In general, the university retains the copyright if it funds a project or if the developer uses an external grant funded through it. Sometimes a granting agency stipulates the conditions of ownership and distribution of returns. It may require a share in the returns, if not outright ownership, or it may prohibit selling the product for profit and require that it be released into the public domain. Many not-for-profit agencies have no restrictions on marketing and distribution as long as they receive no returns themselves; returns would endanger their not-for-profit status.

Work for Hire

An important consideration is whether software development is part of the author's job; if it is, the institution almost always holds the copyright. The California Institute of Technology requires that rights to computer software produced "in line of Institute duty" belong to the institute "regardless of the source of funds used to produce the computer software." In such cases, software development is defined as work made for hire, where, according to the Copyright Act of 1976, "the employer . . . is considered the author" (quoted in Van Arsdale 141). Employees are performing work for hire when their work falls within the "scope of employment"– that is, when the employer exercises supervision and control over it. This doctrine assumes that the software is produced for the employer, at the employer's impetus, and under the employer's direction (see Van Arsdale 141–46).

The work-for-hire doctrine is ambiguous when applied to academic publication. Legally, scholarship is construed as work for hire, even though universities have traditionally allowed faculty members to retain ownership of their publications. While it has been argued that computer programs devised as tools for scholarship are not themselves scholarly work and therefore outside the university's control, programs written for teaching are regarded as scholarship and thus fall within the scope of employment. (Whether writing computer programs constitutes scholarship is itself a controversial issue. See Bourque; Holdstein, "Politics.") According to the work-for-hire concept, then, faculty-developed courseware is the legal property of the university (Van Arsdale 149).

In practice, however, universities frequently apply this concept in reverse: they allow authors ownership of courseware but retain the rights to noninstructional software. To complicate matters, the courts have interpreted work for hire inconsistently and have placed far heavier weight on the use of university facilities and funds than on the type or purpose of the software in deciding ownership. When applied to academic creation, the doctrine presents additional problems. By assigning income from scholarship to the employer instead of to the author, the work-for-hire doctrine conflicts with academic tradition. By defining "author" as employer, the doctrine also contradicts the purpose of copyright – to protect the creator and encourage individual effort. According to one legal writer:

> The underlying purposes of the doctrine are distorted when applied to faculty writings in general, and professors' computer programs, specifically. . . . A court may be forced to choose between abrogating academic tradition or finding the work-for-hire doctrine unconstitutional (Van Arsdale 166).

Universities have tried to circumvent this problem by defining their conditions of work for hire. At the Massachusetts Institute of Technology, instructors who develop software while receiving their regular teaching salary do not necessarily relinquish ownership. The university holds rights only when the salary is paid specifically for software development (3). The Georgia Institute of Technology decides ownership by categorizing development into one of four types: individual efforts, institute-assisted individual efforts, institute-assigned efforts, and sponsor-supported efforts. The institute holds the copyright for software developed as part of the professor's duties, even if the project was not a specific institution assignment. At the same time, it relinquishes rights to instructional software or to software developed by students as part of a class assignment (Bunting 2). Many institutions retain ownership of software developed on released time, for under these circumstances the developer can be said to be hired specifically for this purpose. Sabbaticals are slightly more ambiguous, and some faculty members have been allowed to retain ownership and royalties for software produced while on leave.

Distribution of Returns

Even when the university holds ownership rights, it often shares returns with the developers. In doing so, it provides incentive for faculty members to continue software development. Ownership policies frequently include arrangements for sharing returns, awarding authors a percentage of net profits – the balance of income after the institution has recovered its expenses for development, licensing, marketing, and legal protection. The author's share varies widely from school to school, but ranges from approximately fifteen to fifty percent, with the remainder divided among the software office, the developer's home department, and other administrative units. At Yale University, for example, the author is entitled to twenty to thirty percent (depending on total amount of royalties earned), the author's department or research unit to thirty percent, and a general research fund to the remaining forty to fifty percent (3).

On most software projects, the "author" is seldom a single person but, more often, a team of three or four (and sometimes as many as fifteen) developers, including junior and senior faculty members, graduate and undergraduate students, staff programmers, and outside design or testing consultants. Most policies assume that faculty members – especially senior faculty members – are the creative force in the project, that they conceive and supervise it, and that other participants chiefly follow their instructions. This assumption is based on perceived roles: professors are expected to do research as part of their jobs, while staff members and students are most easily imagined assisting with clerical tasks. Although we can all cite variations on this model, the professor is usually expected to make the major intellectual contribution and therefore receive the royalties. It has not been customary to compensate undergraduate assistants and staff programmers beyond their hourly wage or monthly salary because their participation is most often construed as work for hire. Similarly, student developers who receive course credit for their work rarely receive royalties. Their contribution is considered secondary to their primary role in the project – to learn. Stanford University's policy, for example, normally excludes student programmers from returns (Bunting 4).

This model of scholarly production frequently falls short of actual experience, in which team efforts are likely to blur roles. Programmers and assistants have collaborated with faculty members on design and evaluation, far exceeding their jobs as technicians charged with carrying out someone else's ideas. Junior faculty members who work closely with undergraduates have dominated courseware projects run by full professors who had less contact with the product's audience. And although most of us sign on student programmers because they cost less than professionals and are readily accessible (often they show up in our classes), many of us have relied on their creative advice. As prospective users, students offer an invaluable perspective.

To accommodate these contingencies, many universities have tried to be flexible. Some institutions will award royalties to staff members and student authors if an agreement is made in advance. The difficulty here is that individual participation can change as a project takes shape, with new people joining the team and original participants dropping out. In addition, any one person's contribution can change in unexpected ways. In one project, an outside consultant became thoroughly involved in the project's design and ended up as one of the authors. As the courseware evolves, developers may realize that they need expertise they hadn't counted on. Furthermore, as in any collaborative effort, contribution can be unequal. Sometimes an author will be called upon to work on the project – testing or debugging it, writing additional documentation, assisting users – long after the publisher has acquired the program and the other authors have taken leave of it. Ideally, such cases are decided individually. In 1985, the University of California, Los Angeles, lacking a software ownership policy, awarded a percentage of returns to a staff programmer who, it was argued, had made a "unique contribution" to the software's development.

The complexities of ownership and royalty distribution have led some institutions to provide broad guidelines and decide idiosyncratic projects separately. The policy at Harvard Medical School allows faculty members to own software they develop, but specifies that many projects – those using extensive institutional resources, for example – will be decided case by case (11–12). Flexibility is essential here because software development rarely proceeds according to formula. Developers often combine university and personal resources. One professor used her institution's hardware but paid programmers out of her own pocket; she was allowed to retain the copyright. Some faculty members work partly at home on their own computers and partly at school. Because most writing courseware is being developed on and for microcomputers, more and more instructors are likely to be using their own hardware as well as the institution's. And even when instructors work primarily at home, their courseware development is likely to overlap with their teaching. What better place to test educational software than in the classroom? Ownership and royalty decisions are further complicated when an outside publisher furnishes resources. One professor developed her software on released time the school paid for, but used programmers hired by her publisher. Her school retained ownership, but they split the returns fifty-fifty.

When it comes to royalty distribution, many professors have chosen to share their returns with assistants the university did not recognize – either because they wanted to reward an intellectual contribution or, more often, because they believed that all contributors should share in the profits. One professor, who worked on his own time and without university facilities, is sharing returns according to a three-way division of labor: contribution of the concept, the scripts, and the programming. He is responsible for the concept and scripts and will receive two-thirds of the returns, while his programmer is entitled to the remaining one-third.

Whatever the distribution arrangements, it is important for developers to be aware of their schools' policies at the outset of their projects. In the humanities, lucrative development projects are unusual, and many of us aren't used to thinking about selling our creations. Many professors began by designing courseware for their own students and didn't plan to market it until it generated public interest. Authors who remain ignorant of their schools' policies can find themselves party to ownership and royalty arrangements they are uncomfortable with and that cause bad feeling. One author, who described himself as "burned" on a project, resolved never to design software at his university, and set up his own company. At another school, discord among the developers over who had contributed what caused hostility and a shared conviction that no one had been compensated fairly. Conflict over ownership can extend beyond bad feeling. In some cases, it has stalled plans for licensing and publishing and even interfered with development. At one university, a student copyrighted a program he wrote for an ongoing research project and required the other researchers to pay him a fee to use it (Peterson 188). In another confrontation over ownership, a California Institute of Technology professor went to court, where he was allowed to reclaim his copyright by quitting his job. He resigned from the institute ("Tempest" 86).

Effect of Ownership Rights on Software

The issue here is not just equity – although that is important – but the quality of the finished product and the success of the licensing and distribution methods that accompany it. Someone must choose and negotiate with a publisher, deciding policies for packaging, pricing, copy protection, product support and follow-up, companion products like workbooks and tapes, further refinements, and continued development. These elements profoundly affect the quality of the software, and several of them – pricing and copy protection, for example – are highly controversial. Universities, publishers, and developers often have conflicting needs and interests and may well differ in their intentions for the product. These differences are especially noticeable when it comes to copy protection (see Schwartz, in this volume, for a detailed discussion of copy protection). Many authors are loath to protect their software from unauthorized copying because such schemes interfere with the program's functioning. The more impenetrable the program is to the copier, the more inconvenient (and sometimes the more unreliable) it is for the legitimate user. This is a particular problem for courseware, which is designed for novices and depends on ease of use and minimal reliance on manuals. At the same time, publishers, whose business is selling, are threatened by undercover distribution and require methods of controlling piracy. In one case in which the university owned the software and then sold it to a publisher, the author had to accept a copy protection scheme he opposed on principle. On top of that, his institution had made an agreement with the publisher that obligated him to install the copy protection. (Those who oppose copy protection believe it encourages rather than inhibits piracy. Many programmers consider it a challenge to undermine the scheme and become heroes among their peers when they succeed. Critics of copy protection argue that this attitude is not just counterproductive but also psychologically destructive in that it teaches students to admire piracy [Arms 11].)

Because ownership confers control over the software, the owner determines what the final product looks like and how it will be marketed. Although authors who do not retain ownership may lose control over the software, many publishers have involved authors in marketing decisions. The authors' familiarity with the code as well as with the software's purposes and limitations makes it logical for authors to do final debugging, write documentation and instructor's guides, and add enhancements. They can even help with marketing: in testing the software, they have learned what level of student gets the best use out of it, how it can be used most effectively, and what kind of support student and faculty users may need.

Setting Policy

Because courseware development is fairly new, many schools do not have policies to decide these issues. Several have had to make up policies as they went along, worrying all the way about setting a precedent they might regret. One university's intellectual property administrator has proposed a software office to review each project at the outset of development and at strategic points along the way and to adjust policy for each project. Faculty developers would coordinate their work with the office, which, in turn, would handle publishing and marketing and determine the contribution of project members. The office would draw up a separate agreement for each project. Although the office would follow general guidelines, it would have the flexibility to decide how to apply the guidelines in each case.

Such an arrangement would minimize discord. If courseware ever becomes big business, however, humanities professors will have to grapple with ethical questions their counterparts in engineering and the sciences are now confronting: Should a university or its faculty members profit from academic projects, and to what extent do the university's or the professors' commercial ties conflict with their responsibility to teaching? Some researchers, like Brian Reid at Stanford, believe that the profit motive distorts their research. Others, like Roger Schank at Yale, argue that creative professors who are prevented from profiting from their work will leave academia for industry ("Tempest" 87–90).

By tradition, academics share their work freely, as contributors to one large enterprise – the expansion of knowledge. Many university ownership policies state that their primary goal is to carry out the mission of the university: to ensure the generation and dissemination of knowledge. They justify the financial reward as a means of encouraging faculty members to develop innovative projects. Carnegie Mellon's policy outlines these goals:

- To create a University environment that encourages the generation of new knowledge by faculty, staff, and students.
- To facilitate wide transfer of useful inventions and writings to society.
- To motivate the development and dissemination of intellectual property by providing appropriate financial rewards to creators and the University, and administrative assistance to creators.
- To ensure that the financial return from the development of intellectual property does not distort decisions and operations of the University in a manner contrary to the mission of the University. (1)

It is this concern with the "mission of the University" that troubles critics of academic profit making. For the most part, though, their concern has applied to large-scale projects – usually designed for mainframe and minicomputers – and in departments like chemistry or computer science, where business ties are more frequent and more lucrative than in the humanities. Rarely do these critics address software that is strictly educational.

The trend in courseware seems to be toward making the product as widely available as inexpensively as possible. Because of the difficulties in providing copy protection for software, more and more developers are offering their work for free or at minimal cost. Iowa State University has set up the Clearinghouse for Academic Software to distribute, inexpensively, software developed for Digital Equipment Corporation's Vax minicomputer ("Software Clearinghouse" 28). This not-for-profit center is meant to encourage schools to share the software they develop. Similarly, one chain of copy shops distributes Apple II and Macintosh courseware for the price of duplication plus any royalty the author wants to add on. The goal is "to promote the exchange of computing solutions from instructor to student, campus to campus, across the nation" (*Kinko's* i). The chain recommends that authors keep their software inexpensive to make it as widely available as possible. Unlike most commercial software, academic courseware is sold in fairly low volume and at prices modest enough to attract students ("Academic Courseware"). Much of it is distributed free, especially if it is developed through grants that restrict the authors from collecting royalties. As a result, more and more educational software is being released into the public domain as "freeware."

How much courseware is distributed this way will undoubtedly depend on the courseware itself. Certainly, software that requires extensive hardware and several years to develop is less likely to be given away than smaller, less elaborate programs, but both types will continue to be developed. Large research universities derive much of their income and prestige from major projects and have a stake in encouraging them. At the same time, the availability of microcomputers has encouraged professors to try their hand at relatively simple, easily portable programs, often for specific classroom assignments. Because of the wide range in complexity, size, and purpose – from Stanford's *Would-Be Gentleman* to Carnegie Mellon's *Andrew*[3] – there is probably room for everyone to profit – not just in royalties but in more rewarding teaching and more effective learning.

Notes

[1] I am grateful to Patricia Brennan, intellectual property administrator at UCLA, for her help in providing materials for this article, and also to the faculty software developers and electronic publishers who shared their time and their stories with me. They are, of course, in no way responsible for this essay or for any errors it may contain.

[2] For a full discussion of the nature of software as engineering device or written code and of the question of whether it should be protected under patent or copyright, see Davidson.

[3] *The Would-Be Gentleman* is a game of life in seventeenth-century France, in which the user makes economic and social decisions as an upwardly mobile bourgeois. It runs on a microcomputer – a Macintosh with 128K. *Andrew* is a large instructional network that

incorporates a powerful word processor and electronic mail system. It requires enormous memory, disk storage, and speed.

APPENDIX

Carnegie Mellon Intellectual Property Policy

Organizational Announcement No. 307

Office of the President

July 30, 1985

Carnegie-Mellon University

Subject: Intellectual Property Policy

To: Campus Community

1. Purpose

The Policy reflects the following goals:

- To create a University environment that encourages the generation of new knowledge by faculty, staff, and students.
- To facilitate wide transfer of useful inventions and writings to society.
- To motivate the development and dissemination of intellectual property by providing appropriate financial rewards to creators and the University, and administrative assistance to creators.
- To ensure that the financial return from the development of intellectual property does not distort decisions and operations of the University in a manner contrary to the mission of the University.

The Policy is based upon the following principles relating the University to society:

- The mission of the University remains the generation and dissemination of knowledge.
- Intellectual property will be generated within the University, and there exists an obligation to disseminate it.
- An interface is needed if better technology transfer is to be achieved, and the University will provide mechanisms for that function.[1]

The Policy is based upon the following principles relating faculty, staff, and students to the University:

- Intellectual property is created by individuals or by groups of individuals, who are entitled to choose the course of disclosure: academic freedom of individuals is a higher priority than possible financial rewards.
- There exists a historical tradition allowing authors to retain ownership of intellectual property rights from textbooks and works of art.
- The University is the support of the whole campus community, and is thereby entitled to share in financial rewards.
- There should be incentives for all parties to pursue financial rewards together, consistent with the expressed goals of the Policy. The distribution of these rewards should reflect, insofar as possible, the creative contributions of the creator, and the resources contributed by and risks assumed by both the creator and the University in developing intellectual property.
- Since it is frequently difficult to meaningfully assess risks, resources, and potential rewards, negotiated agreements are to be encouraged whenever possible.

---

[1]This document presumes the existence of a University office to facilitate technology transfer. Such an office would serve as a clearinghouse for contacts with outside partners, would perform patent and copyright tasks, and would develop an effective marketing capability.

2. Definitions

Certain terms are used in this document with specific meanings, as defined in this section. These definitions do not necessarily conform to customary usage.

Intellectual property includes any patentable invention, any copyrightable subject matter, or trade secret. It also includes works of art, and inventions or creations that might normally be developed on a proprietary basis.

University means Carnegie-Mellon University.

Student means any full-time or part-time graduate or undergraduate student, regardless of whether the student receives financial aid from the University or from outside sources. It is the responsibility of students who are also employees of other outside entities to resolve any conflicts between this policy and provisions of agreements with their employers prior to beginning any undertaking at the University that will involve the development of intellectual property.

Faculty means members of the University's Faculty Organization as defined in the Faculty Handbook, plus instructors and special faculty appointments (even in the first year), and part-time faculty.

Staff means any employee of the University other than students and faculty as defined above. If a student is also a part-time University employee, he is considered as staff with regard to intellectual property developed as a result of his employment, and as a student with regard to other intellectual property. A full-time non-faculty employee who is also taking one or more courses is considered to be staff. Visitors to the University who make substantial use of University resources are considered as staff with respect to any intellectual property arising from such use. (The distinction between faculty and staff does not affect intellectual property rights except for representation on the Intellectual Property Adjudication Committee [see Section 5].)

Creator means any person or persons who create an item of intellectual property.

Net proceeds to the University means all proceeds received by the University on intellectual property that it assigns, sells, or licenses, minus any application, litigation, interference, or marketing costs directly attributable to the intellectual property being licensed. Deducted costs shall be reasonable and fair, and shall be properly disclosed; the sources and amounts of compensation shall also be properly disclosed.

Net proceeds to the creator means all proceeds received by the creator from intellectual property owned by him that he sells, assigns, or licenses, less the costs of application, legal protection, or litigation, interference, travel, and other marketing costs directly attributable to the intellectual property being exploited. Such net proceeds do not include compensation legitimately received by the creator for consulting services or interest or other return on invested labor or capital. Deducted costs shall be reasonable and fair, and shall be properly disclosed; the sources and amounts of compensation shall also be properly disclosed.

Substantial use of University facilities means extensive unreimbursed use of major University laboratory, studio, or computational facilities, or human resources. The use of these facilities must be important to the creation of the intellectual property; merely incidental use of a facility does not constitute substantial use, nor does extensive use of a facility commonly available to all faculty or professional staff (such as libraries and offices), nor does extensive use of a specialized facility for routine tasks. Use will be considered "extensive" and facilities will be considered "major" if similar use of similar facilities would cost the creator more than $5,000 (five thousand dollars) in constant 1984 dollars if purchased or leased in the public market. Creators wishing to directly reimburse the University for the use of its facilities must make arrangements to do so before the level of facilities usage for a particular intellectual property becomes substantial. (This provision is not intended to override any other department or University policy concerning reimbursement for facilities usage.)

In General:

In any given year the equivalent figure for a particular amount of money in constant 1984 dollars will be obtained by multiplying that amount of money by the ratio of the most recent quarterly Disposable Personal Income Deflator divided by the average monthly Disposable Personal Income Deflator for the year 1984.

As used in this policy, the masculine gender includes the feminine gender, singular or plural, wherever appropriate.

3. Policy Provisions

This section states the policies concerning ownership of intellectual property created at the University. In order of precedence, ownership of intellectual property shall be as follows:

3-1. Externally Sponsored Work

Ownership Provisions: Intellectual property created as a result of work conducted under an agreement between an external sponsor and the University that specifies the ownership of such intellectual property shall be owned as specified in said agreement. If the University declares itself to be a sponsor, but does not declare itself to be the owner of the intellectual property, ownership shall be determined in accordance with 3-6-4 below.

Procedural Provisions: It is the responsibility of the Research Contracts Office of the University to inform each person whose intellectual property rights are limited by an externally sponsored contract of the intellectual property provisions of that contract in advance of the beginning of work thereon. Such notice is to be in writing and the University may require written acknowledgment of such provisions by any person working on externally sponsored projects. A summary of external sponsorship agreements limiting the intellectual property rights of potential creators will be maintained by the Research Contracts Office and will be available to the general University community.

If the University fails to notify a creator, effectively and in advance, of limitations imposed on his intellectual property rights by external sponsorship agreements, the creator is entitled to receive from the University 50% (fifty percent) of the net proceeds to the University resulting from his intellectual property.

3-2. Internally Sponsored Work

Ownership Provisions: When the University provides funds or facilities for a particular project to the extent of substantial use, it may also choose to designate itself as sponsor of that work. The University may declare itself the owner of intellectual property resulting from said work. In such cases the University must specify in advance the disposition of any intellectual property rights arising from the project. If the University declares itself to be a sponsor, but does not declare itself the owner of the intellectual property, ownership shall be determined in accordance with 3-6-4 below.

Procedural Provisions: It is the responsibility of the Research Contracts Office of the University to inform each person whose intellectual property rights are limited by internally sponsored work of the intellectual property ownership rights specified by the University as to that work in advance of the beginning of work thereon. Such notice is to be in writing and the University may require written acknowledgment of such provisions by any person working on internally sponsored projects. A summary of work for which University sponsorship limits the intellectual property rights of potential creators will be maintained by the Research Contracts Office and will be available to the general University community.

If the University fails to notify a creator, effectively and in advance, of limitations imposed on his intellectual property rights by internal University sponsorship, the creator is entitled to receive from the University 50% (fifty percent) of the net proceeds to the University resulting from his intellectual property.

3-3. Individual Agreements

Ownership Provisions: Intellectual property which is the subject of a specific agreement between the University and the creator(s) thereof shall be owned as provided in said agreement. Such agreements by the University and the faculty are encouraged.

Procedural Provisions: Except where limited by external sponsorship agreements, creators and the University may negotiate individual agreements to govern ownership of intellectual property regardless of the applicability of any other provision hereof.

3-4. Intellectual Property Created within Scope of Employment

Ownership Provisions: Intellectual property created by University employees who were employed specifically to produce a particular intellectual property shall be owned by the University if said intellectual property was created within the normal scope of their employment. Faculty are presumed not to be hired to produce a particular intellectual property. On the other hand, computer programs written on the job by staff computer programmers would fall under this provision.

3-5. Public Dedication

Ownership Provisions: Except when limited by subparts 3-1, 3-2, 3-3, or 3-4 above, the creator of any intellectual property may choose to place his or her creation in the public domain. In such cases both the creator and the University waive all ownership rights to said property.

Procedural Provisions: Creators wishing to place their intellectual property in the public domain are responsible for ascertaining that the right to public dedication of that intellectual property is not limited by any external agreement, University sponsorship arrangement, or terms of employment as described in Provisions 3-1, 3-2, or 3-3. The University Provost will provide such a determination in writing upon request by the creator. It is also the creator's responsibility to ensure that disclosure does not include valuable intellectual property owned by others. (This provision does not release the University from its general obligation to notify creators of limitations to intellectual property rights specified in Provisions 3-1 and 3-2.)

To facilitate the actual transfer of knowledge of the intellectual property to the public at large, the creator shall provide the University with a complete description and documentation of the property placed in the public domain, specifically including a copy of the property in the case of printed material, and complete machine-readable source code in the case of software. All such material provided to the University will be placed in the University Library and made available to the public at large. The University will take appropriate action on a regular basis to publicize summary descriptions of intellectual property recently placed in the public domain. The University will also provide any member of the general public copies of such material on a cost-recovery basis.

The provisions of this section do not apply to the normal scholarly or creative publication processes unless the creator intends to waive all proprietary rights to the publication.

In General

Unless governed by subparts 3-1, 3-2, 3-3, 3-4, or 3-5 above, ownership of intellectual property created at the University shall be determined as follows:

3-6-1. Traditional Rights Retained

Ownership Provisions: In keeping with academic traditions at the University, the creator retains all rights to the following types of intellectual property, without limitation: books (including textbooks, educational courseware, articles, non-fiction, novels, poems, musical works, dramatic works including any accompanying music, pantomimes and choreographic works, pictorial, graphic and sculptural works, motion pictures and other similar audio-visual works, and sound recordings, regardless of the level of use of University facilities. This provision does not include computer software (other than educational courseware) or data bases.

Procedural Provisions: The types of intellectual property listed in the preceding paragraph share the attribute that they display information or visual or auditory appearances which are fully revealed to the purchaser or consumer. Thus, for example, source code listings would also be considered within this category. On the other hand, most computer software and data bases do not share this attribute; they are characterized by their capacity to perform tasks. Because of their utilitarian nature, ownership rights with respect thereto are governed by 3-6-3 or 3-6-4. Educational courseware is included in this provision in all cases because of its role in furthering the primary educational mission of the University.

This provision applies regardless of any University sponsorship of the work, and it may be modified only by a specific prior agreement between the creator and the University. The use of University-owned computers and other facilities in the preparation of books and similar works does not alter this provision, though other University policies may limit such use or require reimbursement to the University. Similarly, the use of externally sponsored resources does not alter this provision, unless the creator is effectively notified in advance of such limitations to his rights in accordance with 3-1.

3-6-2. No Substantial Use of University Facilities

Ownership Provisions: The creator owns all intellectual property created without substantial use of University facilities, including intellectual property rights in computer software and data bases.

3-6-3. Substantial Use of University Facilities – No External or Internal Sponsorship

Ownership of intellectual property created with substantial use of University facilities, but not directly arising from externally sponsored work, or from work for which the University has declared itself as sponsor, shall be determined as set forth hereinafter depending on whether the creator or the University develops said property.

3-6-3-1. Development by Creator

Ownership Provisions: The creator originally owns intellectual property created with substantial use of University facilities but no external or internal sponsorship, and retains said ownership by commercial development of said property subject to the following: (i) the University shall receive 15% (fifteen percent) of the net proceeds to the creator above $25,000 (twenty-five thousand dollars) in constant 1984 dollars from all sources (in the case of patents and copyrights, this provision shall be limited to the life of the patent or copyright), and (ii) the University shall receive a perpetual, non-exclusive, non-transferrable, royalty-free license to use said intellectual property. In the case of software, this license includes access by specified University personnel to the source listings, and the University shall require each person to whom a disclosure is made to execute in advance a binding confidentiality agreement in favor of and enforceable by the creator. If the intellectual property is created solely by a student or students, the creator is exempt from the obligation to pay to the University a fraction of his net proceeds, but not from the provision of this paragraph for a non-exclusive license to the University.

Procedural Provisions: If the creator develops an intellectual property that is covered by this provision, he must make full and fair disclosure to the University of all such sources of compensation relating to that intellectual property.

3-6-3-2. Development by the University

Ownership Provisions: When intellectual property is created with substantial use of University facilities, but not directly arising from sponsored research, the creator will originally retain the rights to the property, provided that he desires to commercially develop the property himself or to make it available to the public. If, however, the creator elects not to commercially develop same or fails to show diligence in pursuing such development, then the ownership rights to that property may be acquired by the University. Intellectual property acquired by the University in this fashion will be treated as in 3-6-4-1 below.

Procedural Provisions: At the time the intellectual property is disclosed to the University's Provost as required under Section 4-1, or at any time thereafter, the University may request that the creator decide whether he will develop the intellectual property or will grant the rights to the University, and execute documents to pass on the title. Such a decision must be made within one year of the request or the creator will automatically lose his rights in favor of the University.

3-6-4. Substantial Use of University Facilities – External or Internal Sponsorship

Ownership of intellectual property created with substantial use of University facilities and directly arising from work sponsored under an agreement between an external sponsor and the University, or from work for which the University has declared itself a sponsor, but for which neither the external sponsor nor the University has specified the ownership of resulting intellectual property, shall be determined as set forth hereinafter depending on whether the creator or the University develops said property.

3-6-4-1. Development by University

Ownership Provisions: The University originally owns intellectual property created with substantial use of University facilities provided by an external agreement or internal University sponsorship and retains said ownership by commercial development of said property, subject to the following: in all cases, the creator shall receive 50% (fifty percent) of the net proceeds to the University.

Procedural Provisions: When an intellectual property is created with substantial use of University resources provided by an external research contract or a specific University sponsorship agreement, and when that contract or agreement either does not specify the disposition of the intellectual property rights arising from that sponsorship, or it permits the University and/or creator to retain or acquire such intellectual property rights, the University will originally retain the rights to such intellectual property.

3-6-4-2. Development by Creator

Ownership Provisions: When intellectual property is created with substantial use of University facilities provided by external or internal sponsorship, the University will originally retain the rights to the property, provided that it desires to commercially develop the property or to make it available to the public. If, however, the University elects not to commercially develop same or fails to show diligence in such development, the ownership rights to that property may be acquired by the creator. Intellectual property acquired by the creator in this fashion will be treated as in 3-6-3-1 above. This assignment of rights to the creator may be prohibited by the terms of an external sponsorship agreement with the University or by an internal University sponsorship declaration, but in such cases the creator must be notified in advance, as in Provisions 3-1 and 3-2.

Procedural Provisions: At the time the intellectual property is disclosed to the University's Provost as required by Section 4-1, or at any time thereafter, the creator may request that the University decide whether it will commercially develop the intellectual property or execute an assignment of the intellectual property rights to the creator. Such a decision must be made within 120 (one hundred twenty) days of the request or the University automatically waives its rights in favor of the creator, and it must execute an assignment of these rights to the creator.

3-6-5. Consulting Agreements

Ownership Provisions: Work done by individuals as consultants to outside firms is presumed not to involve unreimbursed substantial use of University facilities, and the rights to intellectual property created under consulting agreements are retained by the outside firms or the individual as specified by the terms of the consulting agreement and the terms of Provision 3-6-2 above.

Procedural Provisions: Under University policy consulting work must not make substantial unreimbursed use of University facilities except by explicit prior agreement. Any member of the University community who is engaged in consulting work or in business is responsible for ensuring that provisions in his agreements are not in conflict with this policy of the University or with the University's commitments. The University's office for technology licensing will, upon request, provide assistance in this respect. The University's rights and the individual's obligations to the University are in no way abrogated or limited by the terms of such agreements. Each creator of intellectual property should make his obligations to the University clear to those with whom he makes such agreements and should ensure that they are provided with a current statement of the University's intellectual property policy. Appropriate sample contract wording to cover various possible external consulting arrangements shall be available from the University Provost.

4. General Procedures

4-1. The creator of any intellectual property that is or might be owned by the University under this policy is required to make reasonably prompt written disclosure of the work to the University's Provost, and to execute any document deemed necessary to perfect legal rights in the University and enable the University to file patent applications and applications for copyright registration when appropriate. This disclosure to the Provost should be made at the time when legal protection for the creation is contemplated, and it must be made before the intellectual property is sold, used for profit, or disclosed to the public.

Whenever legal protection for intellectual property is anticipated, all persons engaged in such creative activity are encouraged to keep regular notebooks and records.

4-2. Whenever the University undertakes commercial development it shall do so, if possible, in a fashion that provides for the widest possible dissemination, avoiding suppression of inventions from which the public might otherwise benefit, providing for non-exclusive licensing at reasonable royalties, and giving consideration to more favorable or royalty-free licensing to non-profit charitable institutions, minority businesses, or enterprises in developing countries.

4-3. The University's share of any proceeds under this policy will be used to reimburse the University for its expenses for commercial development of intellectual property. Any additional return to the University will be used to further the academic purposes of all the disciplines of the entire University.

5. Resolution of Disputes
This policy constitutes an understanding which is binding on the University and on the faculty, staff, and students upon whom it is effective according to the terms of Section 6 below, as a condition for participating in research programs at the University or for use of university funding or facilities.

Any question of interpretation or claim arising out of or relating to this policy, or dispute as to ownership rights of intellectual property under this policy, will be settled by the following procedure:

1. The issue must first be submitted to the University's Intellectual Property Adjudication Committee in the form of a letter setting forth the grievance or issue to be resolved. The committee will review the matter and then advise the parties of its decision within 60 days of submission of the letter.

2. If any of the parties to the dispute is not satisfied with the committee's decision, the party may seek binding arbitration in Pittsburgh, Pennsylvania and in accordance with the Rules of the American Arbitration Association then in effect. Judgment upon the award rendered by the arbitrator(s) may be entered in any court having jurisdiction thereof. The arbitrator(s) will give some weight to the decision of the Intellectual Property Adjudication Committee in reaching a decision. The losing party of the arbitration hearing will pay for all costs of the arbitration unless the arbitrator(s) specifies otherwise.

The Intellectual Property Adjudication Committee will consist of a Chairman who is a member of the tenured faculty, four other members of the faculty, and four other members representing, respectively, the University administration, the technical staff, and the graduate and undergraduate student bodies. Initially, half of the members of the committee (including the Chairman) will be appointed for two-year terms of office, and the remaining half will be appointed for a one-year term. After one year new members of the Committee will be appointed for two-year terms of office. The Chairman will be appointed by the Chairman of the Faculty Senate, with the advice and consent of the Faculty Senate Executive Committee, and the remaining eight members of the committee will be appointed by the President of the University or his designee. At all times at least one of the faculty members will have had significant practical experience with intellectual property development and exploitation. The faculty members appointed by the President of the University will be selected from a list of nominees prepared by the Faculty Senate or its designated committee, and nominees with experience in intellectual property development will be identified as such by the Faculty Senate. The staff representative will be selected from a list of nominees prepared by Staff Council, and the administration representative will be named directly by the President of the University or his designee. The graduate student representative will be selected from a list of nominees prepared by the Graduate Student Organization. The undergraduate representative will be chosen from a list of nominees prepared by the Student Senate. The Committee will use the guidelines set forth in this policy to decide upon a fair resolution of any dispute.

If possible, the Committee will also provide on request informal advisory opinions to creators and the University indicating how it is likely to interpret the provisions of this policy as it applies to special cases.

6. Effective Date of Policy
This policy will become effective August 27, 1985. Once effective this policy will be binding on new faculty, administration, and staff when hired, and on graduate and undergraduate students when admitted. Current faculty and staff will also become bound by this policy when they sign new employment contracts as the result of the renewal of limited-term appointments or promotion. Other University personnel, including tenured faculty, and current staff and students may choose to become bound by this policy for future and pending intellectual property by voluntary written consent. Unless the creator and the University agree to a different arrangement, intellectual property that is already partially developed at the time this policy becomes effective will be treated according to the provisions of the patent policy by which the creator is currently bound. Similarly, members of the University working under contracts signed before the effective date of this policy who do not choose to accept this policy will remain bound by the patent policies that already apply to them.

With respect to intellectual property developed during the course of employment at the University, this policy shall continue to be binding on any person whose relationship with the University becomes terminated.

The University should take all administrative steps necessary to ensure that employees and students sign, upon initial employment, registration, or at other appropriate times, forms that indicate their acceptance of this policy.

7. Amendments of the Policy
Amendments of this policy may be proposed by the Faculty Senate, Staff Council, or University Administration. Proposed amendments must be approved by a two-thirds majority of votes in the Faculty Senate and subsequently approved by a simple majority of votes cast in a referendum administered by the Faculty Senate that is open to all members of the faculty as defined by this policy and to the exempt staff, provided that this majority constitutes at least 25% (twenty-five percent) of those eligible to vote. This referendum must be preceded by an opportunity for public discussion open to all interested faculty, administration, staff, and students. Amendments that are supported by the faculty and staff must then be approved by the President of the University and adopted by the University Trustees. Once adopted, amendments will become binding on new faculty, administration, and staff when hired, on existing faculty and staff when they sign new employment contracts, and on graduate and undergraduate students

when admitted. Other University personnel, including tenured faculty, and current staff and students may choose to become bound by this policy for future and pending intellectual property by voluntary written consent. Intellectual property that is already developed or under development at the time that an amendment to the policy is ratified will not be bound by the terms of the amendment without the voluntary written consent of both the creator and the University.

Georgia Tech Software Policy

Introduction
The Georgia Institute of Technology is dedicated to the transfer of knowledge to the public. Inherent in this objective is the need to encourage the development of new and useful intellectual material and to make such work available to appropriate user communities. Because of the growing importance of the electronic computer as a tool for education and research, an important class of intellectual work relates to the development of computer software. Such activities (1) benefit Institute graduate and undergraduate programs; (2) contribute to the professional development and advancement of the staff members involved; (3) enhance the reputation of the Institute; (4) promote the general welfare of the public at large by virtue of the benefits gained from the transfer of this technology.

The Institute acknowledges that the faculty, staff, and students of the Institute (members) regularly develop software that has intellectual and commercial value. It is recognized that software development by Institute members may significantly contribute to both the academic/professional reputation of the Institute and the development and advancement of the individual Institute members. With the increased availability of computers on campus, the opportunities for creating software have grown substantially, resulting in an increasingly complex set of issues being raised. Accordingly, the Georgia Institute of Technology does hereby establish the following policy to encourage software development and the dissemination of software resulting from the efforts of its faculty, staff, and students.

As used in this policy, software is defined to be a sequence of symbols in whatever format, which, when interpreted by a computer[,] cause the computer to perform a prescribed function.

I. Determination of Rights and Equities in Software
Different rights and equities shall apply in the following four instances: (1) Individual efforts; (2) Institute assisted individual efforts; (3) Institute assigned efforts; and (4) sponsor supported efforts.

1. Individual Efforts
The right to market software and retain the income resulting from the licensing of such software produced by members of the Institute shall normally rest with the authors of such software provided that: (1) there is no use of Institute personnel and facilities (unless such facilities are available without charge to the public); (2) the software is not prepared in accordance with the terms of a Georgia Tech contract or grant; (3) the software is not generated by Institute employees while acting in any manner relating to or part of their employment responsibilities or expertise at the Institute, whether or not such development is a specific Institute assignment. Software authors may submit software to the Institute for review, evaluation, and (if it so qualifies) for release which they believe qualifies under this Article as an individual effort; provided, the failure to submit any software for review and evaluation or the failure of the Institute to require any disclosure shall not be construed to be a waiver of any rights held by the Institute in or to software which does not qualify for release.

2. Institute Assisted Individual Efforts
Rights to software produced by members of the Institute shall vest with the Institute where there is any support of the individual's effort or use of Institute personnel and facilities. The Institute shall make a reasonably prompt determination as set forth in Par. II-2 below of its interest in out-licensing such software or retaining its right to utilize such software in its re-

search and education programs. If the Institute determines that it desires to out-license the software, the division of royalty income from such out-licensing shall be as set forth in Par. II-3 below. If the Institute determines that it does not want to out-license the software, then it may by appropriate contract provide for the division of royalty and other matters or release its rights therein to the authors, provided the release does not conflict with any outstanding Institute commitments. Any such release will be subject to retention by the Institute of a non-exclusive, royalty-free license for use of such software by the Institute for research and educational purposes.

3. Institute Assigned Efforts

Rights to software produced by members of the Institute shall vest with the Institute if the Institute has assigned the task of producing the software. The Institute shall make a reasonably prompt determination as set forth in Par. II-2 below of its interest in out-licensing such software or retaining the right to utilize such software internally. If the Institute determines that it desires to out-license the software, then the division of royalty income shall be determined as set forth in Par. II-3 below. If the Institute determines that it is not economically feasible to out-license the software, then it may release its rights to the authors if such release does not conflict with any outstanding Institute commitments. Any such release will be subject to retention by the Institute of a non-exclusive, royalty-free license for use of such software by the Institute for research and educational purposes.

4. Sponsor Supported Efforts

Rights to software developed as a result of work supported partially or fully by an external agency through a contract or grant to the Institute shall be governed by the terms of the contract or grant. In cases where such rights are shared between the sponsor and the Institute, the authors may appropriately share in the license royalty income (excluding income from sale or patent and data rights). The nature and extent of such royalty sharing shall be determined as set forth in Par. II-3 below.

II. Administrative Procedures

1. Software Committee

The Vice President for Research at the Institute shall administer these policies utilizing the services of the Institute Software Committee as described herein. The Software Committee shall consist of nine members appointed by the President for three-year staggered terms, two of whom shall be the Vice President for Business and Finance and the Associate Vice President for Graduate Studies and Research. The Chairperson shall be designated by the President. A member of the staff of the Vice President for Research, designated by him, and the Assistant to the President for Information Technology shall be ex-officio, non-voting members of the Committee. Five members (excluding ex-officio members) shall constitute a quorum. The committee shall meet at the call of the Chairman and shall act in an advisory capacity to the Vice President for Research in matters relating to the rights, equities, use and disposition of software developed by the members of the Institute.

2. Determinations

The Software Committee shall determine and recommend to the Vice President for Research the classification of and rights and equities in any software developed by members of the Institute. Where such rights are determined to reside wholly or in part with the Institute, the Vice President for Research, in consultation with the Vice President for Business and Finance, shall determine whether the Institute wishes to out-license the software. The goal will be to make such determinations within 90 days after the receipt of the software and adequate supporting documentation by the Vice President for Research.

3. Royalty Income from Software (Guidelines)

In making its determinations the Software committee shall take into consideration the following guidelines: Of the net royalty income received by the Institute from the out-licensing of any software, fifteen percent of such royalty income shall be distributed to the member or members who developed the software and/or made a substantive contribution to the commercialization of the software. Net royalty income is defined to be gross royalty income received by the Institute after deduction for agent or sponsor fees, legal expenses, administrative expenses and other direct or indirect costs relative to the software in question, as determined by the Vice President for Research in consultation with the Vice President for Business and Finance. The member(s) who may be entitled to a portion of the royalty income received by the Institute shall normally be designated by the Vice President for Research, upon consultation with the Institute members involved in the development of the software; provided, the Vice President for Research may also utilize the services of the Software Committee in making such determinations. At least thirty-five percent of the net royalty received shall be returned to the unit in which the software was developed for continued software development and maintenance – provided that the unit presents and implements acceptable plans for the use of such funds. All awards of royalty distribution from software out-licensing to members of the Institute will cease when the member's connection with the Institute ceases, except for reasons of death, disability, retirement, or graduation, or exceptional circumstances as determined by the Vice President for Research and confirmed by the Software Committee. If exceptional circumstances exist, distributions may continue for no longer than three years after the members' connection with the Institute has ceased. Thereafter, such members' royalties shall be paid to the Institute.

4. Routine Cases
In routine cases where the authors and the Vice President for Research agree as to the classification of said rights and equities in submitted software, royalties may be allocated in keeping with the guidelines as set forth above.

5. Non-routine Cases
All disputed cases shall be referred to the Software Committee for its written recommendations with respect to the classification of and rights and equities in submitted software before final decision by the Vice President for Research.

6. Changes in Policy
Changes in this policy may be made upon the recommendation of the Software Committee with the approval of the Vice President for Research, and the President, and shall be submitted to the Chancellor for his approval and that of the Board of Regents.

7. Duties of Institute Members
In order to assure that the rights and equities of the parties are determined in a prompt and timely manner, and in order to preclude unnecessary expenditures of resources, Institute members shall disclose in writing to the Vice President for Research, in sufficient detail to enable a thorough review and evaluation, any computer software generated in whole or in part by such members during the term of their employment or attendance at the Institute. Provided, software generated by Institute members solely for the purpose or function of classroom instruction within the Institute or as a student assignment for an Institute course need not be disclosed if such software is not utilized for any other purpose. It shall be a further obligation of each Institute member to maintain the confidentiality of any computer software disclosed or to treat it in accordance with the intellectual property protection mechanism implemented by the Institute, as designated by the Institute. The Vice President for Research shall be responsible for providing advice and assistance in software development and related matters. Those responsible for carrying out programs that may generate software with full or partial support of the Institute or a sponsor shall consult in advance with the Vice President for Research concerning any questions regarding ownership, out-licensing, or disposition of such software.

The Institute may at its discretion and under directive of the Vice President for Research, utilize any protective mechanisms it deems appropriate for both physical protection of software covered by this policy and protection of the Institute's rights to said software and royalty income therefrom.

8. Implementation
In the implementation of this policy, the Vice President for Research may, with the approval of the President and the Chancellor, contract with the Georgia Tech Research Corporation

or other non-profit organizations for the development and management of its software licensing program. A copy of the executed contract (licensing agreement) shall be forwarded to the Chancellor.

9. Appeals and Conflicts

Institute members shall have the right to appeal decisions of the Vice President for Research to the President of the Institute. Institute personnel may, in accordance with Article IX of the Bylaws of the Board of Regents, apply to the Board of Regents for a review of the decision of the President. In the event of a conflict between this policy and any policy of the Board of Regents, the latter shall prevail.

Computers and Writing Research: Shifting Our "Governing Gaze"

Andrea W. Herrmann

———◆———

As a writing tool, the computer brings with it radical changes in the lives of writers, editors, teachers, and students. Despite intense research into the effects of computers on writers and writing over the last several years, we have not received a clear perception of the complex issues involved, including the role the computer plays in the teaching of writing and the impact it has had on writing classrooms.

Like its parent, writing research, computers-and-writing research has essentially failed to look at writing from a social point of view. We have generally analyzed parts of writing in isolation from their contexts: texts or parts of texts, an individual's composing or revising processes, or the effects of a particular software program. Instead of searching for more global understandings of the writing event, including the context in which it occurs, scholars engaged in computers-and-writing research have generally sought a particle view. While such research can provide useful information, too frequently the parts do not add up to a coherent whole. The existing research offers only a glimpse of the human and social implications that the use of computers entails. Findings do little toward assisting teachers in creating effective pedagogical applications.

I explore in this article what I perceive to be pressing matters. I maintain that research methods for investigating the impact of computers on writers should encompass the larger social perspective of writers working within various discourse communities. The importance of social context in understanding writers has come about as a result of contributions from anthropology and sociolinguistics, as well as from the field of writing. Consequently, writing researchers are modifying, even radically rethinking, what they expect their research to tell them and the methods they use. There appears to be a shifting emphasis from quantitative research to qualitative designs, including the use of ethnography. As a result, we have gained a clearer view of the changes that are occurring within our writing environments, including changes in the social relationships among writers. In many ways computers-and-writing research has followed in the footsteps of the larger field of writing research. To understand why computers-and-writing research must emulate research methods that are sensitive to context and social issues, it will help to see why writing research has moved in that direction.

An Overview of Writing Research in General

Analyses of writing research take one of two fundamental perspectives: either a look at the *how* of it – that is, the nature of the methodologies employed – or an examination of the *what* of it – that is, the nature of the objects under study. Over the last two decades, there has been a substantial shift in both the way writing research is conducted and the subjects researchers choose to investigate. These areas, as I will argue further on, interrelate. To understand the connections, we must look first at the historical shifts that have occurred in research methodology and then at similar shifts in the objects being studied. Finally, we will examine the questions that writing researchers ask, since such inquiries play a decisive role in the *how* and the *what* of the research process.

Inquiry Paradigms and Investigative Categories

Some researchers, such as Richard Young and Maxine Hairston ("Winds of Change"), adapting Thomas Kuhn's theory of scientific revolutions in the hard sciences to the humanities, have heralded the changes in the field of composition as a "paradigm shift." Others, including Robert Connors and Stephen M. North (318–21), question whether composition has ever had a paradigmatic structure and, therefore, challenge the notion of a paradigm shift. Whether we accept or reject the occurrence of a paradigm shift, the plurality of models in writing research is evident. As North points out, writing researchers fall into one of four groups: experimentalists, clinicians, formalists, and ethnographers. Experimentalists "seek to discover generalizable 'laws' which can account for – and, ideally, predict – the ways in which people do, teach, and learn writing"; the clinicians, for their part, focus on individuals and conduct case studies, while the formalists "build models or simulations" to study the "formal" properties of phenomena; and the ethnographers, who are concerned with "people as members of communities," produce "narrative accounts of what happens in those communities" (137).

As with shifts in methodology, there have been substantial alterations in the types of subjects chosen to be studied. We can group the objects under investigation in composition research into three categories, using Lester Faigley's terminology: the textual perspective, the individual perspective, and the social perspective ("Nonacademic Writing"). The textual perspective, as the term suggests, looks at aspects of the written text. By contrast, the individual perspective shifts attention from the text to the writer's conception of the writing task (235).

And, finally, the social perspective views communication and, therefore, writing, as "inextricably bound up in the culture of a specific society" (236). Faigley states that

> researchers taking a social perspective study how individual acts of communication define, organize, and maintain social groups. They view written texts not as detached objects possessing meaning on their own, but as links in communicative chains, with their meaning emerging from their relationships to previous texts and the present context. (235)

Kenneth A. Bruffee has traced the history of the social construction of knowledge through multiple disciplines. He credits Kuhn's idea that scientific knowledge is a social construct as the "spark" for social constructionist thought and indicates that Richard Rorty extended Kuhn's idea to encompass all knowledge ("Social Construction" 774). Bruffee deemphasizes the individual's role and highlights the group and its language interactions in creating meaning: "Social construction assumes that the matrix of thought is not the individual self but some community of knowledgeable peers and the vernacular language of that community" (777). Bruffee views language as a means by which humans join and participate in communities (784). Language is no longer a conduit that exists on "the margin of knowledge"; it becomes, rather, "the center of our understanding of knowledge," thereby placing reading and writing at the center of education (778).

As with the relation of language to knowledge, so the questions researchers ask should be viewed not as peripheral to research efforts but at their center. Research questions, more than any other factor, determine the how and the what of research. Making connections between research questions, methodologies, and objects of study in the parent field of composition research provides a useful framework for understanding the shifts taking place in computers-and-writing research.

Making Connections

Research questions greatly influence what researchers select to observe – the objects of study – and how they choose to observe them – the methodology. The questions have changed over time, as writing researchers reassessed the assumptions underlying their approaches and the focal point of their research interest. Questions have gone from a narrow focus – for instance, what happens to a particular written product when the writer is subjected to certain conditions – to broader concerns – what happens to writers learning or working within a particular context. Historically, the nature of the inquiry paradigms and the objects under study have changed in response to the changing research questions.

The first shift, as we have noted earlier, was away from a textual perspective, with its emphasis on the analysis of written products, to an individual perspective, with its increased interest in composing processes. Accompanying this shift was a change from quantitative, experimental research designs, intended to measure how texts improved, to qualitative, descriptive research designs, whose purpose was to observe writers at work. Instead of positing traditional cause-and-effect questions, researchers began to ask, "What is this student's writing process?" and they conducted case studies to find out. Classroom methods changed, too, as teachers, who formerly had seen their role as simply to assign and grade writing, now assisted students in prewriting, drafting, and revising during the process of writing. As our research questions continued to broaden, our research designs became increasingly inclusive. Other questions raised were "What is going on in this writing classroom?" and "What are the patterns of interaction among the participants?" These new questions spawned a second shift, which took place during the second half of the 1980s, concerning the what and how of composition research. As a result of this change in perspective, qualitative researchers have enlarged their focus from case studies, often conducted without sensitivity to social context, to studies that observe individuals within groups and within specific contexts. The emphasis is no longer on one writer's cognitive processes but on writers working or learning within a particular community. The movement is away from context-free case studies and toward context-sensitive ethnographies, an approach that encompasses the social perspective. And, as before, classroom practices have changed, too. The amount of teacher-centered activities directed at the entire class has decreased in favor of peer group collaboration.

It should be noted that case-study research may be viewed either within the qualitative tradition, as case-study researchers usually view themselves, or within the positivistic or quantitative tradition, as North views them. How one views case studies determines whether one sees writing research as self-destructing or as leading to growth. Case studies for North (his clinical mode) represent "compromises" within the positivist tradition (138). Further, he believes that writing research methods should not be considered a "unified response to some shared paradigmatic crisis" (321); rather, they are in a warlike condition. This is because, according to North, methodological differences over how knowledge is made can create "insurmountable barriers" (365). Therefore, he believes, the field of "composition as a knowledge-making society is gradually pulling itself apart" (364). A more optimistic assessment is to view case studies as a logical link between experimental research, on the one hand, and ethnographic research, on the other. In my opinion, case studies and research involving models or simulations represent stepping-stones in the historical stream of writing research. They form an important bridge between traditional, quantitative research, at one extreme of the continuum, and qualitative, ethnographic designs, at the other. Thus I view composition research, including computers-and-writing research, not as pulling itself apart but as reshaping and redefining its methodological approach, broadening its focus from a reliance on narrow questions and positivistic research traditions to embrace wider questions and qualitative techniques. It becomes, from this perspective, a movement that encourages the observations of individuals' behavior patterns within groups and over time. In my view, case-study writing research developed in response to the limitations of experimental research, including the inability to investigate in-depth the learning processes of individuals. Moving from a purely quantitative tradition to one that encompasses qualitative approaches requires the researcher to embrace a new perspective on the nature of knowledge.

Janet Emig refers to an individual's way of seeing as a "governing gaze" and believes that researchers generally use methods that reflect their overall governing gaze ("Inquiry Paradigms" 65). Because the changing nature of research questions has spawned more context-sensitive studies, an increasing number of writing researchers appear to be shifting their governing gaze. The notion of a governing gaze has implications for both the methodology and the content of writing research and of computers-and-writing research.

An Overview of Computers-and-Writing Research

As a discipline, computers and writing has learned important lessons from the parent field of writing. Many of the early studies involving computers and writing, just like the earliest research in composition, tended to emphasize written products and to ignore the social context created by writers working within a community. Increasingly, however, computers-and-writing researchers are shifting from a reliance on traditional experimental approaches, primarily concerned with textual perspectives, to the use of descriptive designs that capture individual and social perspectives. The reason that many of the earliest studies of computers and writing were experimental may stem largely from the nature of the research questions that were asked. At the risk of oversimplifying the matter, we can say that the question at the foundation of much of the work, either implicitly or explicitly, was whether or not computers, particularly in the form of word processors, made writing better.

Analyzing Written Texts

Inspired, perhaps, by a desire to find simple answers, researchers conducting early studies of word processing and writing often looked at students' before-and-after texts in order to measure writing improvement. Gail E. Hawisher, in her first review of writing and word-processing research, "Studies in Word Processing," examined various features of twenty-four such investigations. She noted that many of the studies looked at texts in terms of the number of words, the number of errors, the frequency and types of revision, and the quality of the finished products. Certainly information of this sort can be helpful. Yet the process of analyzing written texts according to selected features involves troubling assumptions. Can we really assume that writing quality is related to length? Isn't shorter just as likely to be better, since it is generally difficult to write short pieces well? Relying on counts of revision to suggest writing progress is also problematic. Can surface features, such as dangling modifiers, faulty parallelism, or illogically coordinated sentences, be accurately quantified? Even though researchers may use the same instrument (and we assume it is an instrument that measures what it claims to measure), problems may still exist with the findings. Hawisher points out, for example, that although five studies used Faigley and Witte's revision taxonomy, these same studies did not report their findings according to Faigley and Witte's terms, making their conclusions not comparable (18). But should we assume that quantification of the actual revision done on two separate assignments, even when the quantification is conducted systematically and according to some hierarchy of priorities, represents an accurate barometer of writing growth or of the value of using computers for writing?

There are good reasons why our research has not yet adequately addressed the question of whether word processing leads to better writing. The question is not a simple one, although much of our research treats it that way. Do we want to know whether the student's writing was instantly transformed by the computer's magic wand into something "better" than it used to be? This question assumes a straightforward view of things; the answer will be either "yes" or "no." The effect of the computer on writers and writing is either "good" or "bad." The assumption is frequently made, as we said, that an analysis of the students before-and-after texts will tell the story. Moreover, the confidence our research exhibits concerning our ability to analyze written texts may be unearned. Our gross measures do not yet permit a complete picture that accurately depicts writing growth. There is sparse information to suggest the degree of importance among linguistic features in the development of writing skills or to indicate the patterns of change that presumably take place in the writer's ability to manipulate these linguistic features over time, culminating in writing maturity. When we focus on error or the quantity of revisions rather than on the presence of quality, we contribute, I believe, to the creation of a particle view that distorts the multiplicity of factors involved in good writing. While our research has yet to establish an appropriate scale for judging written products, the measures that we intuitively know to be more significant are usually ignored. We should include, among other things, the writer's control over global discourse strategies involving content, focus, organization, and audience; the writer's ability to use arguments, details, and examples effectively for a particular audience; the writer's level of syntactic fluency; and the writer's appropriate use of cohesive devices. If the writing moves us, that should count for something, too. Understanding the role such features play in the creation of a written text is frequently impossible without a comprehensive understanding of the writer and the context in which the writing developed.

Observing Individuals

As with writing research in general, computers-and-writing research eventually shifted focus from a textual to an individual perspective. A growing number of researchers chose to investigate writers' cognitive processes by a case-study approach. In an analysis of forty-two examples of research in computers and writing, Hawisher indicates that eleven were case studies ("Research and Recommendations"). Many case studies in writing research do not attempt to capture students in their natural context; the same can be said of case studies involving writers using word processing. Such case studies often occur in laboratory-like settings where the writers are asked to compose under unusual circumstances: sitting in a special room with the researcher present; writing on an assigned topic with the researcher as the audience, rather than for real communicative reasons; composing while simultaneously verbalizing their thoughts aloud; and working under researcher-imposed time constraints. It may be true that, in spite of the artificiality of the writing situations – perhaps in part because of them – the case studies may produce a wealth of detailed information. Sometimes they permit researchers and practitioners to look at writing in important new ways. However, we certainly must question the value of computers-and-writing research that exposes individuals to unique or highly stressful writing conditions and then evaluates how the students perform. And sometimes subjects are introduced in a cursory fashion to a computer and a word-processing program (or some other writing-related software) and within a short time evaluated to determine whether improvements in their before-and-after compositions could be detected.

Research assumptions appear to be that first-time users are not intimidated by the new technology; that they do not need more than a superficial orientation to use the computer hardware; that they do not need word-processing instruction, no matter how complex the program; and that the research conditions do not create stress that interferes with the composing process. Furthermore, many studies assume that transformations in the students' texts, including improvement in writing quality, will take place soon after students begin to use the computer equipment. As our experiences teaching students who are learning to write with computers increasingly show, however, there is little basis for these assumptions. Instead of hoping for the magic-wand results frequently expected of computer use in classrooms – a mystical transformation from "bad writing" to "good writing" – we should look for another kind of student learning. We should ask whether, after instruction, students have become more engaged by the process of writing; have acquired more sophisticated techniques for composing, revising, and editing; and have begun to integrate their expanding repertoire of word-processing skills into their composing processes. What particular challenges and obstacles has the electronic environment presented to the learners? How do they resolve them? What role does software other than word processing play in student writing? When we ask these questions, we acknowledge the need for detailed information on the teacher's pedagogical strategies; on the role relationships of the participants; and on the various points of view of the students and teacher, including descriptions of how students interact and write collaboratively. The issue of evaluating writers, their texts, and their growth in writing ability is complex. As Lillian Bridwell and Richard Beach state, "If we cannot accurately describe the mature writer or the mature text, we have tremendous difficulty describing their characteristics as they emerge or evolve" (12).

There is still another drawback to studies of writing with word processing that focus on individuals: most of the investigations do not attempt to capture writing in a particular social context. While they may describe the physical environment, most case studies do not present systematically gathered data concerning face-to-face interactions with colleagues or peers. For instance, no descriptions of students reading and commenting on one another's texts, asking questions, challenging, assisting, or planning collaboratively are included. In short, these studies often do not reveal how the writing evolved as a result of the writer's intentions; contact with other media, such as literature, film, newspapers, or television; or relationships with other individuals.

Describing Writers within Social Contexts

Researchers and teachers increasingly understand that the process of writing is a creative and social, as well as individual, endeavor. As Bridwell and Beach state:

> What is needed to guide future research is a model for writing production that represents a more global view of the factors affecting writers. A primary assumption of this model should be that we cannot isolate writing from the social, political, and psychological context in which it occurs. (6)

Deborah Brandt also strongly advocates an awareness of context in studies of writing. She has written extensively on the relationship of context to writing research; her works include "Text and Context" and "Toward an Understanding of Context in Composition." She points out the importance of context in understanding the significance of what writers do when they write. Brandt refers to this unexplored area in research as "the dark stage upon which a writer's plans and thoughts and language are played out" ("Toward an Understanding" 140). While theorists such as Bridwell, Beach, and Brandt call for the inclusion of context in writing research in general, other researchers stress the need for research into the effects of computers within pedagogical contexts. Cynthia L. Selfe and Billie J. Wahlstrom suggest an increase in classroom studies to create a more accurate picture of the relationship between computers and the teaching of writing ("Computers and Writing"). According to Deborah H. Holdstein and Tim Redman, a goal of research and pedagogy must be to seek methods that actually work for students (53). One of Hawisher's conclusions emphasizes the need for more research on the effects of the computer and word processing in the writing class ("Studies in Word Processing" 23–24).

Capturing Social Change in the Computer Classroom

As researchers, we have begun to question our myopic attention to texts and individuals. One of the most exciting features of classrooms using computers is their potential for changing learning into a more holistic, collaborative, and student-centered endeavor. Contrary to the earliest fears that computers might isolate children, research is beginning to demonstrate that under certain conditions, computers can create learning that is more egalitarian and collaborative (Bernhardt and Appleby 35–38; Daiute, "Patterns"; Herrmann, *Using the Computer* 212–20;

Selfe and Wahlstrom, "Emerging Rhetoric"). In other words, computers hold forth the promise of contributing to the creation of environments in which students exercise greater control over what they learn and how they learn it.

Such transformations, while possible, do not happen automatically. Schools reflect the social conditions of the larger society (Wilcox 453). Even when computer access is equitable – for example, within a classroom of highly motivated students and teacher – powerful constraints may serve to exacerbate the socioeconomic divisions in the larger community and mirrored by the school (Herrmann, "Ethnographic Study" 83). Success is not simply a matter of bringing in the computers and turning the students loose. Initiating change in the school environment is a complex process. Participants – teachers, students, administrators, and even parents – must agree to the use of the technology and to explorations involving innovative applications. The participants must negotiate rules and adapt to changing expectations. According to Selfe, teaching writing with computers without a reconsideration of our goals as literacy educators will not improve the opportunities of those who are socially and politically disadvantaged. The "marginalization of individuals because of race, age, gender, and handicap" and the "unequal distribution of power within economic and social groups" will continue ("Computer-Supported" 1–2). While technology potentially has the ability to provide tools to empower students, it "holds hands with a tradition in which such empowerment has not been the agenda," according to Glynda A. Hull (16). It is not simply a question of getting students to adapt to the technology but rather of using research to develop technological applications designed to fit the needs of underprepared students.

The empowerment of all students, including the disenfranchised, depends on research approaches that describe what is happening among the participants within the teaching-learning context. What factors contribute to or hinder the creation of collaborative writing environments? What factors make it easy or difficult for underprepared students to learn to use computers in writing classrooms? To understand the multitude of issues reflecting our current pedagogical interests requires us to reconsider our earlier, narrowly focused research approaches, in favor of the broader insights afforded by context-sensitive, descriptive research, particularly ethnography. Descriptive research is sometimes poorly understood by the people the researcher hopes to communicate with – teachers, theoreticians, other researchers, administrators, editors of journals, and the public at large. For some it is considered less "scientific" than experimental approaches. Yet if writers working in electronic environments are to be studied from a social perspective, we must shift our governing gaze from the quantitative orientation that has historically dominated computers-and-writing research to include qualitative approaches. The reevaluation requires of those who would conduct such research, as well as those who would read and understand it, a willingness to recognize that specific expertise is required. Carrying out sound descriptive research is as demanding as carrying out sound experimental research, perhaps more so.

Quantitative versus Qualitative Research

It is important for both teachers and investigators interested in computers-and-writing research to grasp the critical differences, particularly at their extremes, between quantitative and qualitative research. The anthropologist Clifford Geertz indicates that the ultimate objective of quantitative research is to find laws, whereas qualitative research seeks to discover meaning (5). Quantitative research focuses on random samples of countable items and looks for statistical significance in order to generalize to other situations; qualitative research looks beyond the overt behavior to the significance of the events for the participants and attempts to reveal the general through an in-depth investigation of the particular (Eisner 7). While in quantitative research the investigator is expected to be neutral and "independent of the observed phenomenon," in qualitative research the investigator is the major instrument of the research (Carini 8–9). The most critical difference between the two approaches, however, lies in the ultimate purpose of the research. While quantitative research tests hypotheses, qualitative research strives to generate hypotheses. To test a hypothesis, the researcher first identifies an aspect of a theory in need of investigation, collects and analyzes the data, and then revises the theory as needed. To discover a hypothesis, in contrast, the researcher identifies a process needing study, collects and analyzes the data, and then generates the hypotheses that lead to the building of new theories (Brause). While it is important to note differences between quantitative and qualitative research approaches, it is equally important to understand that the two techniques need not be viewed as circumscribed entities in opposition to each other. I view quantitative and qualitative studies as stretching across a continuum. At one end is experimental research; at the other is ethnography. Case studies and model or simulation research fall at intervals in the middle. It is not uncommon for researchers to integrate aspects of the various approaches into their designs. Understanding the differing assumptions within each tradition gives investigators the flexibility of creating research, based on the nature of the inquiry, that incorporates the best of each.

Shifting Our Governing Gaze

The final task of computers-and-writing researchers who have shifted their concerns from narrow to broad-based questions that include the social context of writing is to learn how to carry out descriptive research. Fortunately, there are a variety of ways to gain expertise in qualitative research: (1) by reading extensively in the field, particularly the ethnographies and case studies written by successful qualitative researchers; (2) by taking workshops in qualitative approaches offered by colleges and universities; (3) by becoming an apprentice to someone conducting such research; and (4) by designing and carrying out descriptive studies of one's own. Such efforts should be well rewarded professionally. We need qualitative research on teachers and students, in various classroom settings, who are using a variety of computer equipment for writing. Teachers might consider the benefits of becoming researchers in their own classrooms, although such a role is not without its problems (Herrmann, *Using the Computer* 342-45, "Researching Your Own Students"). Another important area of inquiry involves the larger school environment. For example, how available are computers and software for English instruction? What is the system of allocation and what provisions are made to assist English teachers who want to use computers? Still another possibility is qualitative research within teacher education. Such research could identify the computer skills that writing teachers need and useful ways to help teachers acquire them (Herrmann, "Teaching Teachers" 227-28).

If we want to examine the constellation of factors involved in the new discourse communities created by electronic environments, we must reassess our research methods. Rather than confine our studies of writers to texts they produced artificially for the purpose of research, we should conduct research in naturalistic settings like the home, the workplace, and the school. We should also make sure we include the newer contexts created by electronic technology, namely, local-area and wide-area communication networks. (See Spitzer, "Computer Conferencing," for more information on the educational applications of teleconferencing.) We need to understand the microcosm, such as the nuances of oral interactions within electronic contexts that culminate in writing; at the same time, we need to understand the macrocosm through panoramic and longitudinal views of writers in social contexts. We must illuminate the "dark stages" of these contexts, if we hope to learn how technological innovations are changing writers and their work. As we continue to investigate the impact of computers on writers and writing, what is required, finally, is a shift in our governing gaze to include methods of research, such as ethnography, that embrace the social perspective.

Notes on Contributors

Thomas T. Barker is associate professor of English in the Technical Communications Program at Texas Tech University. He has published work in computers and writing and in software documentation in the *Technical Writing Teacher, Computers and Composition, Collegiate Microcomputer,* and the *Journal of Technical Writing and Communication.* He is editor of a book entitled *Perspectives on Software Documentation: Inquiries and Innovations* and is word-processing coordinator for the Texas Project in Writing across the Curriculum. Since 1984 he has been coordinator of the microcomputer classroom in the English department.

David N. Dobrin has been interested in computers and writing ever since he got an account on MIT's Project Athena. Subjects he has written or lectured on include style checkers, spelling checkers, grammar checkers, idea processors, and computer networks. He currently runs a consulting firm in Cambridge, Massachusetts, that specializes in technical manuals and warnings. His book *Writing and Technique* was published by the NCTE in 1989.

Lisa Gerrard is on the faculty of the University of California, Los Angeles, Writing Programs, where, since 1980, she has used mainframe and microcomputers in her teaching. One of the developers of *HBJ Writer* (formerly *Wandah*), Gerrard is the editor of *Writing at Century's End: Essays on Computer-Assisted Composition* and the author of *Writing with* HBJ Writer.

Gail E. Hawisher is on the faculty of Purdue University, where she is also co-editor of *Computers and Composition,* a professional journal for writing teachers. Before receiving a PhD from the University of Illinois, Urbana-Champaign, she was head of the English department at a high school in Columbus, Ohio. Currently she is editing a collection of readings on the teaching of English to be published by State University of New York, Stony Brook, Press. Her articles have appeared in the *English Journal, Research in the Teaching of English,* and *Computers and Composition.*

Andrea W. Herrmann has an EdD in applied linguistics from Teachers College, Columbia University. She is assistant professor and coordinator of graduate studies in the Department of English at the University of Arkansas, Little Rock. She teaches courses in expository writing, writing with computers, methods of teaching writing, and sociolinguistics in the MA program in technical and expository writing. Herrmann has published articles and contributed chapters to books on ethnography, TESOL, and computers and composition.

Deborah H. Holdstein directs the writing program at Governors State University, where she is professor of English and rhetoric. She has served on the Executive Committee and as local chair of the Conference on College Composition and Communication and serves on the editorial boards of several journals; Holdstein regularly makes presentations at the MLA, CCCC, and other conferences and consults widely in the United States. She prepared a textbook on the relation between computers and the writing process, published by Holt, Rinehart and Winston in 1989. Her book *On Composition and Computers* was published in 1987 by the MLA.

Ellen McDaniel is a member of the English department at North Carolina State University, where she teaches technical writing, assists in the humanities computing laboratory, and is supported by a fifty percent research contract with the Technical University of Denmark. McDaniel spent two years as guest researcher at the Technical University in Copenhagen working with computer systems for producing technical and research documentation. Before that, she was assistant professor at Texas A&M University.

Helen J. Schwartz, professor of English at Indiana University, Indianapolis, is author of *Interactive Writing*, articles on computers in writing, and the computer programs *Organize* and *Seen*. Besides chairing the committee on computer use of the CCCC and the MLA, she has headed a national panel of EDUCOM to assess the use of computers in composition and recommend a blueprint for future use of the technology as a teaching tool. Schwartz has consulted widely in the United States, China, Sweden and, as a Fulbright Senior Scholar, the Netherlands; in 1987–88 she was a Dana Fellow at Carnegie Mellon University.

Cynthia L. Selfe lives and works in Houghton, in the Upper Peninsula of Michigan, north of two-thirds of the population of Canada. Selfe teaches at Michigan Technological University, among an active community of scholars in the department of humanities.

Michael Spitzer is currently dean, School of Humanities, New York Institute of Technology, where he formerly chaired the English department. A member of NCTE's Committee on Instructional Technology and chair of the Assembly on Computers in English, he regularly makes presentations on computers and writing at NCTE, CCCC, and other conferences. Spitzer's publications have dealt with computer conferencing and the use of computer networks in the writing classroom.

Works Cited

"Academic Courseware Available." *Wheels for the Mind* 2 (1986): 33–37.

Adams, Hazard S. "How Departments Commit Suicide." *ADE Bulletin* 76 (1983): 7–13.

Adams, Hazard S., and Leroy Searle, eds. *Critical Theory since 1965*. Tallahasee: Florida State UP, 1986.

Anderson, Paul V., R. John Brockmann, and Carolyn R. Miller, eds. *New Essays in Technical and Scientific Communication: Research, Theory, and Practice*. Farmingdale: Baywood, 1983.

Appleby, Bruce C. "Computers and Composition: An Overview." *Focus* 9 (1983): 102–10.

Arms, William Y. "Intellectual Property Rights and Computer Software." *SIGUCCS Newsletter* [Special Interest Group on University and College Computing Services of the Association for Computer Machinery] 15.1 (1985): 8–16.

Axelrod, Joseph. *The University Teacher as Artist*. San Francisco: Jossey-Bass, 1973.

Axelrod, Rise B., and Charles R. Cooper. *Reading Critically, Writing Well*. New York: St. Martin's, 1987.

Barker, Thomas. "Issues in Software Development in Composition." *Computers and Composition* 3 (1986): 53–67.

———. "Studies in Word Processing and Writing." *Computers in the Schools* 4 (1986): 109–21.

Baron, Naomi S. "Humanists among the CRTs: The Problem of Method in the Humanities." *Liberal Education* 71 (1985): 251–63.

Bartholomae, David. "Inventing the University." *When a Writer Can't Write: Studies in Writer's Block and Other Composing Process Problems*. Ed. Mike Rose. New York: Guilford, 1985. 134–65. Also published in *Journal of Basic Writing* 5 (1986): 4–23.

Bator, Robert, and Mitsuru Yamada. *Blue Pencil*. Computer software. Prentice, 1986. IBM.

Batson, Trent. "The ENFI Project: A Networked Classroom Approach to Writing Instruction." *Academic Computing* Feb. 1988: 32–33, 55–56.

Bazerman, Charles. *The Informed Writer*. 2nd ed. Boston: Houghton, 1985.

———. "A Relationship between Reading and Writing: The Conversation Model." *College English* 41 (1980): 656–61.

———. "Scientific Writing as a Social Act: A Review of the Literature of the Sociology of Science." Anderson et al. 156–84.

Bernhardt, Stephen A., and Bruce C. Appleby. "Collaboration in Professional Writing with the Computer: Results of a Survey." *Computers and Composition* 3.1 (1985): 29–42.

Bizzell, Patricia. "What Happens When Basic Writers Come to College?" *College Composition and Communication* 37 (1986): 294–301.

Bleich, David. "Discerning Motives in Language Use." Horner 81–95.

Booth, Wayne C. "The Common Aims That Divide Us: Or, Is There a 'Profession 81'?" *Profession 81* (1981): 13–17.

———. "LITCOMP: Some Rhetoric Addressed to Crypto-Rhetoricians about a Rhetorical Solution to a Rhetorical Problem." Horner 57–80.

———. "Presidential Address: Arts and Scandals 1982." *PMLA* 98 (1983): 312–22.

Bork, Alfred. "Computer Networks for Learning." *T.H.E. Journal* 14.9 (1987): 68–71.

Bourque, Joseph. "Understanding and Evaluating: The Humanist as Computer Specialist." *College English* 45 (1983): 67–73.

Bowen, Betsy, and Jeffrey Schwartz. "What's Next for Computers: Electronic Networks in the Writing Classroom." NCTE convention. San Antonio, Nov. 1986.

Brandt, Deborah. "Text and Context: How Writers Come to Mean." *Functional Approaches to Writing: Research Perspectives.* Ed. Barbara Couture. Norwood: Ablex, 1986. 93–106.

———. "Toward an Understanding of Context in Composition." *Written Communication* 3 (1986): 139–57.

Brause, Rita. "Understanding, Applying and Doing Research in English." NCTE convention. Denver, Nov. 1983.

Bridwell, Lillian, and Richard Beach, eds. *New Directions in Composition Research.* New York: Guilford, 1984.

Bridwell, Lillian, Parker Johnson, and Stephen Brehe. "Composing and Computers: Case Studies of Experienced Writers." *Writing in Real Time: Modelling Production Processes.* Ed. A. Matsuhashi. Norwood: Ablex, 1986. 81–107.

Bridwell, Lillian, Geoffrey Sirc, and Robert Brooke. "Revising and Computing: Case Studies of Student Writers." *The Acquisition of Written Language: Revision and Response.* Ed. Sarah Freedman. Norwood: Ablex, 1985. 721–94.

Bruce, Bertram, Sarah Michaels, and Karen Watson-Gegeo. "How Computers Can Change the Writing Process." *Language Arts* 62 (1985): 143–49.

Bruffee, Kenneth A. "Collaborative Learning and the 'Conversation of Mankind.'" *College English* 46 (1984): 635–52.

———. "Social Construction, Language, and the Authority of Knowledge: A Bibliographic Essay." *College English* 48 (1986): 773–90.

Bunting, Wade A. "A Study of Computer Software Policies and Licensing Practices in Three Major U.S. Universities." Unpublished ms. UCLA Office of Contract and Grant Administration, Intellectual Property Div., 1985.

Burns, Hugh L. "Pandora's Chip: Concerns about Quality CAI." *Pipeline* 6 (1981): 7–9.

———. "Recollections of First-Generation Computer-Assisted Prewriting." Wresch 15–33.

California Institute of Technology. "Royalties and Copyrights." Rev. Pasadena: CIT, 1984.

Carini, Patricia. *Observation and Description: An Alternate Methodology for the Investigation of Human Phenomena.* Grand Forks: U of North Dakota P, 1975.

Carnegie Mellon University, Office of the President. Organization Announcement 307: Intellectual Property Policy. Rev. Pittsburgh: Carnegie Mellon U, 1985.

Carroll, Joyce A. "Process into Product: Teacher Awareness of the Writing Process Affects Students' Written Products." Bridwell and Beach 315–33.

Catano, James. "Computer-Based Writing: Navigating the Fluid Text." *College Composition and Communication* 36 (1985): 309–16.

Cherry, Lorinda L. *Diction. Style. Explain.* Computer software. Bell Labs, 1980. 1–15.

Cherry, Lorinda L., and W. Vesterman. "Writing Tools: The *Style* and *Diction* Programs." *The UNIX User's Guide.* Murray Hill: Bell Labs, 1980. 1–15.

Collier, Richard. "The Word Processor and Revision Strategies." *College Composition and Communication* 34 (1983): 149–55.

Connors, Robert J. "Composition Studies and Science." *College English* 45 (1983): 1–20.

Costanzo, William. "Language, Thinking, and the Culture of Computers." *Language Arts* 62 (1985): 516–23.

Critique [formerly *Epistle*]. Computer software. IBM, 1988.

Cyert, Richard M. "The Impact of Microcomputers on Education." *Perspectives in Computing* 6.2 (1986): 4–8.

Daiute, Colette. "Do 1 and 1 Make 2? Patterns of Influence by Collaborative Authors." *Written Communication* 3 (1986): 382–408.

———. *Writing and Computers*. Reading: Addison, 1985.

Data Relator. Computer software. State of CA. Apple.

Davidson, Duncan M. "Protecting Computer Software: A Comprehensive Analysis." *Jurimetrics Journal* 23 (1983): 337–425.

Deshler, David. "Metaphors and Values in Higher Education." *Academe* 71.6 (1985): 22–28.

DeYoung, Alan J. "Assessing 'Faculty Productivity' in Colleges of Education: Penetration of the Technical Thesis into the Status System of Academe." *Educational Theory* 35 (1985): 411–21.

Diction. *See* Cherry.

Dinan, John S., Rebecca Gagnon, and Jennifer Taylor. "Integrating Computers into the Writing Classroom: Some Guidelines." *Computers and Composition* 3 (1986): 33–39.

Dobrin, David. "Don't Throw Out Your Dictionary Yet." *Righting Words* 1.2 (1987): 8–14.

———. "Is Technical Writing Particularly Objective?" *College English* 47 (1985) 237–51.

———. "Searching for Mr. Goodcheck." *Righting Words* 1.3 (1987): 12–18.

———. "Some Ideas about Idea Processors." Gerrard 95–107.

———. "What's New with Grammar and Style Checkers." *Computers and the Humanities*. Forthcoming.

———. "What's Technical about Technical Writing?" Anderson et al. 227–49.

———. *Writing and Technique*. Urbana: NCTE, 1989.

Dowling, Colette. *The Techno/Peasant Survival Manual*. New York: Bantam, 1980.

Dreyfus, Herbert L. *What Computers Can't Do*. Rev. New York: Harper, 1979.

Eagleton, Terry. *Literary Theory: An Introduction*. Minneapolis: U of Minnesota P, 1983.

Eisner, Elliot W. "On the Differences between Scientific and Artistic Approaches to Qualitative Research." *Educational Researcher* Apr. 1981: 5–9.

Ekman, Richard. "The Feasibility of Higher Education Reform in the Humanities." *Liberal Education* 71 (1985): 273–82.

Elbow, Peter. *Writing without Teachers*. New York: Oxford UP, 1973.

Electronic Ink. Computer software. Science Research Associates, Martin Siegel, author. In progress.

Emig, Janet. *The Composing Processes of Twelfth Graders*. Urbana: NCTE, 1971.

———. "Inquiry Paradigms and Writing." *College Composition and Communication* 33 (1982): 64–75.

———. "Writing as a Mode of Learning." *College Composition and Communication* 28 (1977): 122–28.

Epistle. *See Critique*.

Etchison, C. "Word Processing and the Basic Writer." Conference on College Composition and Communication. St. Louis, 1988.

Explain. *See* Cherry.

Faigley, Lester. "Competing Theories of Process: A Critique and A Proposal." *College English* 48 (1986): 527–42.

———. "Nonacademic Writing: The Social Perspective." Odell and Goswami 231–48.

Faigley, Lester, and Stephen Witte. "Analyzing Revision." *College Composition and Communication* 32 (1981): 400–14.

Feenberg, Andrew. "Network Design: An Operating Manual for Computer Conferencing." *IEEE Transactions on Professional Communication* 29 (1986): 2–7.

Fifth C. Ongoing computer conference sponsored by a grant from the Exxon Education Foundation, on the New York Inst. of Technology conferencing system.

Fish, Stanley. *Is There a Text in This Class? The Authority of Interpretive Communities.* Cambridge: Harvard UP, 1980.

Flower, Linda, and John R. Hayes. "A Cognitive Process Theory of Writing." *College Composition and Communication* 32 (1981): 365–86.

Fodor, Jerry. "Methodological Solipsism Considered as a Research Strategy in Cognitive Science." Haugeland 307–38.

Fredwriter. Computer software. State of CA. Apple.

Geertz, Clifford. *The Interpretation of Cultures: Selected Essays.* New York: Basic, 1973.

Geisler, Cheryl. "A Heirarchy of Word Processing Skills for Writers." U of Pittsburgh Conference on Computers and Writing. Pittsburgh, May 1986.

Gerrard, Lisa, ed. *Writing at Century's End: Theory and Practice in Computers and Writing.* New York: Random, 1986.

Gilbert, Sandra. "What Do Feminist Critics Want? A Postcard from the Volcano." Showalter, *New Feminist* 29–45.

Golub, Jeffrey. Private note on the New York Inst. of Technology conferencing system. 12 June 1987.

Graff, Gerald. *Professing Literature: An Institutional History.* Chicago: U of Chicago P, 1987.

Gunner, Jeanne, and Ed Frankel. *The Course of Ideas.* New York: Harper, 1986.

Hairston, Maxine. "Breaking Our Bonds and Reaffirming Our Connections." *College Composition and Communication* 36 (1985): 272–82.

———. "The Winds of Change: Thomas Kuhn and the Revolution in the Teaching of Writing." *College Composition and Communication* 33 (1982): 76–88.

Halloran, S. M., and A. N. Bradford. "Figures of Speech in the Rhetoric of Science and Technology." *Essays on Classical Rhetoric and Modern Discourse.* Ed. Robert J. Connors, Lisa S. Ede, and Andrea A. Lunsford. Carbondale: Southern Illinois UP, 1984. 179–92.

Haring-Smith, Tory. "Research on Word Processing and Composing: A Critical Survey." U of Pittsburgh Conference on Computers and Writing. Pittsburgh, May 1986.

Harris, Jeanette. "Student Writers and Word Processing: A Preliminary Evaluation." *College Composition and Communication* 36 (1985): 323–30.

Hart, Robert S., and Frank Hodgins. "The Writer's Workbench *Style* Module as a Predictor of Holistic Writing Evaluations." Computers in Writing and Language Instruction Conference. Duluth, 1 Aug. 1988.

Hartman, Geoffrey. *Criticism in the Wilderness: The Study of Literature Today.* New Haven: Yale UP, 1980.

Hartwell, Patrick, with Robert H. Bentley. *Open to Language.* Instructor's manual. New York: Oxford UP, 1982.

Harvard Medical School, Office of Technology Licensing and Industry-Sponsored Research. *Guide to Protecting and Managing Intellectual Property*, 1985.

Hashimoto, I. "Toward a Taxonomy of Scholarly Publication." *College English* 45 (1983): 500–05.

Haugeland, John, ed. *Mind Design.* Cambridge: MIT P, 1981.

Hawisher, Gail E. "The Effects of Word Processing on the Revision Strategies of College Freshmen." *Research in the Teaching of English* 21 (1987): 145-59.

———. "Research and Recommendations for Computers and Composition." *Critical Perspectives on Computers in Composition*. Ed. Gail E. Hawisher and Cynthia L. Selfe. New York: Teachers CP, 1989. 44-69.

———. "Research in Word Processing: Facts and Fictions." U of Pittsburgh Conference on Computers and Writing. Pittsburgh, May 1986.

———. "Studies in Word Processing." *Computers and Composition* 4 (1986): 6-35.

HBJ Writer. Computer software. Harcourt, 1986. IBM.

Herrington, Anne. "Classrooms as Disciplinary Forums for Reasoning and Learning." *College Composition and Communication* 35 (1985): 404-13.

Herrmann, Andrea W. "An Ethnographic Study of a High School Writing Class Using Computers: Marginal, Technically Proficient, and Productive Learners." Gerrard 79-91.

———. "An Interim Report of an Ethnographic Study of a Computers and Writing Class: Collaborative Activities." *Conference on Computers and Writing: New Directions in Teaching and Research*. Ed. Lillian Bridwell and Donald Ross. Minneapolis: U of Minnesota, 1984. 159-73.

———. "Researching Your Own Students: What Happens When the Teacher Turns Ethnographer?" *Writing Instructor* 6 (1987): 114-28.

———. "Teaching Teachers to Use Computers as Writing Tools." *English Education* 20 (1988): 215-29.

———. *Using the Computer as a Writing Tool: Ethnography of a High School Writing Class*. Diss. Teachers C, Columbia U, 1985. Ann Arbor: UMI, 1986. 8602051.

Hillocks, George, Jr. *Research on Written Composition: New Directions for Teaching*. Urbana: ERIC and NCTE, 1986.

———. "What Works in Teaching Composition: A Meta-analysis of Experimental Treatment Studies." *American Journal of Education* Nov. 1984: 133-70.

Holdstein, Deborah H. *On Composition and Computers*. New York: MLA, 1987.

———. "The Politics of CAI and Word-Processing: Some Issues for Faculty and Administrators." Gerrard 122-30.

Holdstein, Deborah H., and Tim Redman. "Empirical Research in Word Processing: Expectations versus Experience." *Computers and Composition* 3.1 (1985): 43-54.

Horner, Winifred B., ed. *Composition and Literature: Bridging the Gap*. Chicago: U of Chicago P, 1983.

Huckin, Thomas. "A Cognitive Approach to Readability." Anderson et al. 90-108.

Huizinga, Johan. *Homo Ludens*. Boston: Beacon, 1970.

Hull, Gloria T., Patrice Bell Scott, and Barbara Smith, eds. *All the Women Are White, All the Blacks Are Men, but Some of Us Are Brave: Black Women's Studies*. Old Westbury: Feminist, 1982.

Hull, Glynda Ann. "Literacy, Technology, and the Underprepared: Notes toward a Framework for Action." *Quarterly* 10.3 (1988): 1-25.

Hull, Glynda Ann, Carolyn Ball, James L. Fox, Lori Levin, and Deborah McCutchen. "Computer Detection of Errors in Natural Language Texts: Some Research on Pattern-Matching." *Computers and the Humanities* 21 (1987): 103-18.

Hunter, Linda. "Basic Writers and the Computer." *Focus* 9 (1983): 89-92.

Iser, Wolfgang. *The Act of Reading: A Theory of Aesthetic Response*. Baltimore: Johns Hopkins UP, 1978.

———. "The Reading Process: A Phenomenological Approach." *Reader-Response Criticism: From Formalism to Structuralism*. Ed. Jane Tompkins. Baltimore: Johns Hopkins UP, 1980. 50–69.

Jacobus, Lee A. *A World of Ideas*. New York: St. Martin's, 1983.

Jay, Paul. Rev. of *Professing Literature*. *Genre* 21 (1988): 118–23.

Jobst, Jack. "Computers and the Obsolete English Teacher." *Focus* 9 (1983): 89–92.

———. "Word Processing: Two Ethical Concerns." *Journal of Technical Writing and Communication* 17.1 (1987): 1–8.

Kantor, Kenneth J. "Classroom Contexts and the Development of Writing Intuitions: An Ethnographic Case Study." Bridwell and Beach 72–94.

Kelly, Derek A. *Documenting Computer Application Systems: Concepts and Techniques*. New York: Petrocelli, 1983.

Kennedy, Mary Lynch. "The Composing Process of College Students Writing from Sources." *Written Communication* 2 (1985): 434–56.

Kidder, Stephen. Write On: The Statewide Telecommunications and Writing Conference. Ongoing computer conference on the New York Inst. of Technology conferencing system.

Kiefer, Kathleen. "Revising on the Word-Processor: What's Happened, What's Ahead." *ADE Bulletin* 87 (1987): 24–27.

———. "Writing: Using the Computer as Tool." Olsen 90–102.

Kinkead, Joyce. "Computer Conversations: E-Mail and Writing Instruction." *College Composition and Communication* 38 (1987): 337–41.

Kinko's Academic Courseware Exchange Catalog. Santa Barbara: Kinko's Service, 1986.

Kolodny, Annette. "Dancing through the Minefield: Some Observations on the Theory, Practice, and Politics of a Feminist Literary Criticism." *Feminist Studies* 6 (1980): 1–25. Rpt. in Adams and Searle 499–512.

Labin, Linda L., and Edward F. Villella. "The Bonding of the Arts and Sciences with the Technologies: A Move to Strengthen Academia." *Educational Technology* 26 (1986): 447–48.

Lanham, Richard, and Michael Cohen. *Homer*. Computer software. Scribner's, 1983. Apple.

Lauer, Janet. "Heuristics and Composition." *College Composition and Communication* 21 (1970): 396–404.

LeFevre, Karen B. *Invention as a Social Act*. Carbondale: Southern Illinois UP, 1987.

Leonard, George. "The Great School Reform Hoax." *Esquire* Apr. 1984: 47–56.

Marcus, Stephen. "Computers and English: Future Tense, Future Perfect?" *English Journal* 76 (1987): 88–90.

———. *Practical Writing Resource Kit*. Lexington: Heath, 1987.

———. "Real-Time Gadgets with Feedback: Special Effects in Computer-Assisted Writing." Wresch 120–30.

Marling, William. "What to Do with Your Computer When You Get It." *Focus* 9 (1983): 48–53.

Martin, Nancy, et al. *Writing and Learning across the Curriculum 11–16*. London: Ward Lock Educational, 1976.

Marvin, Carolyn. "Fables for the Information Age: The Fisherman's Wishes." *Illinois Issues Humanities Essays* 2nd ser. (Sept. 1982): 17–24.

Massachusetts Institute of Technology. Copyright Policy. Rev. Cambridge: MIT, 1985.

McAllister, Carole H. "The Effects of Word Processing on the Quality of Writing: Fact or Illusion." *Computers and Composition* 2 (1985): 36–44.

McCroskey, Mia. "LAN Courseware: New Wave of Products Breaks New Ground." *T.H.E. Journal* 14.9 (1987): 12–14.

McKenzie, Alan T., ed. *A Grin on the Interface: Word Processing for the Academic Humanist.* New York: MLA, 1984.

Meserole, Harrison. "Shakespeare in the Second Age of Science." Lecture at Texas A&M U. College Station, 1985.

"Microlab Facts." *English Microlab Registry* 2 (1986): 2.

Miller, Carolyn. "A Humanistic Rationale for Technical Writing." *College English* 40 (1979): 610–17.

Minsky, Martin. "A Framework for Representing Knowledge." *The Psychology of Computer Vision.* Ed. Patrick Winston. New York: McGraw, 1975. 211–77.

———. "Thinking Machines." *Technology Review* Oct. 1984: 42–60.

Modern Language Association. "*MLA Bibliography* on Compact Disc." *MLA Newsletter* 19.3 (1987): 17–18.

Moffett, James. *Teaching the Universe of Discourse.* Boston: Houghton, 1968.

Moses, Ingrid. "Promotion of Academic Staff: Reward and Incentive." *Higher Education* 15.1–2 (1986): 135–49.

Murray, Donald M. "Teaching the Other Self: The Writer's First Reader." *College Composition and Communication* 33 (1982): 140–47.

———. "Teach Writing as Process Not Product." *Leaflet* Nov. 1972: 11–14.

National Task Force on Educational Technology. "Transforming American Education: Reducing the Risk to the Nation." *T.H.E. Journal* Aug. 1986: 58–67.

Nelson, Cary. "Canon Formation and Literary History: Toward Discursive Antagonism." Address. MLA convention. San Francisco, Dec. 1987.

North, Stephen M. *The Making of Knowledge in Composition: Portrait of An Emerging Field.* Upper Montclair: Boynton/Cook, 1987.

Odell, Lee. "Beyond the Text: Relations between Writing and Social Context." Odell and Goswami 249–80.

Odell, Lee, and Dixie Goswami, eds. *Writing in Nonacademic Settings.* New York: Guilford, 1987.

Ohmann, Richard. "Literacy, Technology, and Monopoly Capital." *College English* 47 (1985): 675–89.

Olsen, Solveig. *Computer-Aided Instruction in the Humanities.* New York: MLA, 1985.

Parson, Gail. *The Writing Process and the Microcomputer.* Urbana: NCTE, 1985.

Perl, Sondra. "Understanding Composing." *College Composition and Communication* 31 (1980): 363–69.

Perl, Sondra, and Nancy Wilson. *Through Teachers' Eyes: Portraits of Writing Teachers at Work.* Portsmouth: Heinemann, 1987.

Peterson, Ivars. "Bits of Ownership." *Science News* Sept. 1985: 188–90.

Peyton, Joy K., and Sarah Michaelson. "The ENFI Project at Gallaudet University: Focus on Teacher Approaches and Reactions, 1986–87 School Year." Unpublished report, 1987.

Porter, James E. "Intertextuality and the Discourse Community." *Rhetoric Review* 5 (1986): 34–47.

Prose. Computer software. McGraw, 1988. Macintosh.

Reisman, Bernard. "Performance Evaluation for Tenured Faculty: Issues and Research." *Liberal Education* 72 (1986): 73–87.

Robinson, Jay L. "Literacy in the Department of English." *College English* 47 (1985): 482–98.

Robinson, Lillian S. "Treason Our Text: Feminist Challenges to Literary Criticism." *Tulsa Studies in Women's Literature* (1983). Rpt. in Adams and Searle 572–82.

Rodrigues, Dawn, and Raymond J. Rodrigues. *Teaching Writing with a Word Processor, Grades 7–13.* Urbana: NCTE, 1986.

Rodrigues, Raymond. "Moving Away from Writing Process Worship." *English Journal* 74 (1985): 24–27.

Rogers, Al, and Barbara Miller-Souviney. "Effective School Networking: The San Diego School Networking Project. A Practical Approach." San Diego County Office of Education. Unpublished ms., 1986.

Rollins, Mark. "Coming of Age with Computers: One Department's Experience." *Focus* 9 (1983): 54–58.

Rosenblatt, Louise. *The Reader, the Text, the Poem: The Transactional Theory of the Literary Work.* Carbondale: Southern Illinois UP, 1978.

Ross, Donald, and Lillian S. Bridwell. "Computer-Aided Composing: Gaps in the Software." Olsen 103–15.

Schwartz, Helen J. *Interactive Writing: Composing with a Word Processor.* Textbook, disk, and teacher's manual. New York: Holt, 1985.

———. "Monsters and Mentors: Computer Applications for Humanistic Education." *College English* 44 (1982): 141–52.

———. *Seen.* Computer software. Conduit, 1988. Apple, IBM.

———. "*Seen*: A Tutorial and User Network for Hypothesis Testing." Wresch 47–62.

Schwartz, Helen J., and Louis J. Nachman. *Organize.* Computer software. Wadsworth, 1988. Apple IIe with 128K, IBM for MS-DOS 3.0+, disks.

Selfe, Cynthia L. *Computer-Assisted Instruction in Composition: Create Your Own!* Urbana: NCTE, 1986.

———. "Computer-Supported Writers' Conferences: Feminism, Marxism, Collaboration, Revolution." Unpublished ms., 1988.

———. "Creating a Computer Lab That Teachers of Composition Can Live With." *Collegiate Microcomputer* 5.2 (1987): 149–58.

———. "Dancing on the Cutting Edge: English Teachers and Computers." *Focus* 9 (1983): 80–88.

Selfe, Cynthia L., and Gail Hawisher, eds. *Critical Perspectives on Computers and Composition.* New York: Teachers CP, 1989.

Selfe, Cynthia L., and Billie J. Wahlstrom. "An Emerging Rhetoric of Collaboration: Computers, Collaboration and the Composing Process." *Collegiate Microcomputer* 4 (1986): 289–95.

———. "Computers and Writing: Casting a Broader Net with Theory and Research." *Computers and the Humanities* 22 (1988): 57–66.

———. "The Benevolent Beast: Computer-Assisted Instruction in the Teaching of Writing." *Writing Instructor* 2 (1983): 183–92.

Selzer, Jack. "What Constitutes a 'Readable' Technical Style?" Anderson et al. 71–89.

Showalter, Elaine, ed. *The New Feminist Criticism: Essays on Women, Literature, and Theory.* New York: Pantheon, 1985.

———. "Feminist Criticism in the Wilderness." Showalter 243–70.

Sirc, Geoffrey M. "Learning to Write on a LAN." *T.H.E. Journal* 15.8 (1988): 99–104.

Skubikowski, Kathleen, and John Elder. "Word Processing in a Community of Writers." *College Composition and Communication* 38 (1987): 198–201.

Slaughter, Sheila. "From Serving Students to Serving the Economy: Changing Expectations of Faculty Role Performance." *Higher Education* 14.1 (1985): 41–56.

"Software Clearinghouse Established at Iowa State." *Technological Horizons in Education* 14 (1986): 28.

Spatt, Brenda. *Writing from Sources*. New York: St. Martin's, 1983.

Spitzer, Michael. "Computer Conferencing: An Emerging Technology." Selfe and Hawisher 187–200.

———. "Writing Style in Computer Conferences." *IEEE Transactions on Professional Communication* 29 (1986): 19–22.

Standiford, Sally N., Kathleen Jaycox, and Anne Auten. *Computers in the English Classroom*. Urbana: NCTE, 1983.

Stephenson, Dwight W. "Two-Point-Five Cheers: The Computers Are Coming." *Focus* 9 (1983): 37–43.

Strassmann, Peter A. "Information Systems and Literacy." *Literacy for Life*. Ed. Richard W. Bailey and Robin Melanie Fosheim. New York: MLA, 1983. 115–21.

Style. See Cherry.

Sudol, Ronald A. *Textfiles: A Rhetoric for Word Processing*. New York: Harcourt, 1987.

Swarts, Heidi, Linda S. Flower, and John R. Hayes. "Designing Protocol Studies of the Writing Process: An Introduction." Bridwell and Beach 53–71.

Tamplin, John. "Penn State Enjoys Success with On-Line Editor." *Electronic Education* Jan. 1986: 10–16.

"The Tempest Raging over Profit-Minded Professors." *Business Week* 7 Nov. 1983: 86–88.

Thompson, Diane P. "Teaching Writing on a Local Area Network." *T.H.E. Journal* 15.2 (1987): 92–97.

Tierney, Robert J. "Writer-Reader Transactions: Defining the Dimensions of Negotiation." *Forum: Essays on Theory and Practice in the Teaching of Writing*. Ed. Patricia L. Stock. Upper Montclair: Boynton/Cook, 1983. 147–51.

Turkle, Sherry. *The Second Self: Computers and the Human Spirit*. New York: Simon, 1984.

Turner, Judith Axler. " 'Latin Skills' Software Earns a Profit for Authors at U. of Delaware." *Chronicle of Higher Education* 27 Nov. 1985: 24.

Vacca, JoAnne, and Anthony Manna. "Professional Growth of Secondary English Teachers." *English Education* 17 (1985): 162–70.

Van Arsdale, Cory H. "Computer Programs and Other Faculty Writings under the Work-for-Hire Doctrine: Who Owns the Intellectual's Property?" *Santa Clara Computer and High-Technology Law Journal* 1 (1985): 141–67.

VanDeWeghe, Richard. "Research in Composition and the Design of Writing Programs." *ADE Bulletin* 61 (1979): 28–31.

Weizenbaum, Joseph. "Not without Us: A Challenge to Computer Professionals to Bring the Present Insanity to a Halt." *Fellowship* 52.10–11 (1986): 8–10.

Westcott, Edward. *David Harum: A Story of American Life*. New York: Appleton, 1931.

Wilcox, Cathleen. "Ethnography as a Methodology and Its Application to the Study of Schooling: A Review." *Doing the Ethnography of Schooling: Educational Anthropology in Action*. Ed. George Spindler. New York: CBS College Publishing, 1982. 456–88.

Winkler, Victoria. "The Role of Models in Technical and Scientific Writing." Anderson et al. 111–22.

Winston, Patrick. Personal communication. 13 Mar. 1984.

Woodruff, Earl, Mary Bryson, Peter Lindsay, and Elana Joram. "Some Cognitive Effects of Word Processors on Enriched and Average Eighth Graders." Annual meeting of the American Educational Research Assn. San Francisco, Apr. 1986.

Woolpy, Jerome H. "Delphi: A Computer Program Featuring Dialogue among Students and between Students and the Instructor." *Collegiate Microcomputer* 3 (1985): 157–62, 178.

Wresch, William, ed. *The Computer in Composition Instruction: A Writer's Tool.* Urbana: NCTE, 1984.

———. *Writer's Helper.* Computer software. Conduit, 1986. IBM, Apple.

Writing Is Thinking. Computer software. Kapstrom, 1984. IBM.

Yale University. Patent Policy. Rev. New Haven: Yale U, 1984.

Young, Arthur. "Rebuilding Community in the English Department." *ADE Bulletin* 77 (1984): 13–21.

Young, Richard E. "Paradigms and Problems: Needed Research in Rhetorical Invention." *Research on Composing: Points of Departure.* Ed. Charles C. Cooper and Lee Odell. Urbana: NCTE, 1987. 29–48.

Young, Richard E., A. L. Becker, and Kenneth L. Pike. *Rhetoric: Discovery and Change.* New York: Harcourt, 1970.

Index